THE FLYING SCOTSMAN

THE FLYING SCOTSMAN

THE ERIC LIDDELL STORY

SALLY MAGNUSSON

For Siggy and my father

First published 1981
This edition first published 2007

STADIA is an imprint of
Tempus Publishing Limited
Cirencester Road, Chalford,
Stroud, Gloucestershire, GL6 8PE
www.tempus-publishing.com

British Library Cataloguing in Publication Data.
A catalogue record for this book is available from the British Library.

ISBN 978 0 7524 4352 2

Typesetting and origination by Tempus Publishing Limited
Printed and bound in Great Britain

Contents

Acknowledgements

The main research for this book was carried out for the first edition in 1981 and drawn from a variety of sources, ranging from contemporary newspaper articles and standard reference books to interviews with members of Eric Liddell's family and others who knew him personally. Although many are no longer alive today, I remain grateful to them all, and to Stan Greenberg, sports statistician, for meticulously checking the details of Liddell's career as a runner.

The books I found most helpful and illuminating were: Annie Buchan, *Adventure in Faith*; Neil Campbell, *The Story of Edinburgh University Athletic Club*; Brian Catchpole, *A Map History of Modern China*; Norman Cliff, *Courtyard of the Happy Way*; Langdon Gilkey, *Shantung Compound: The Story of Men and Women under Pressure*; Tom McNab, *Actors to Athletes: The Making of Chariots of Fire* (unpublished) and *The Complete Book of Athletics*; Revd D.P. Thomson, *Scotland's Greatest Athlete*; Mary Wang and Edward England, *Stephen the Chinese Pastor*; and Melvyn Watman, *History of British Athletics*.

In revising and updating the book I have had the benefit of additional information in David McCasland's comprehensively researched *Eric Liddell: Pure Gold* (Discovery House, 2001) and David Michell's personal account of his internment at Weihsien, *A Boy's War* (OMF Books, 1988). I am grateful to both these authors for their insights. My thanks also to Eric's eldest daughter, Patricia Russell, for taking the time in the middle of moving house and continent to check the manuscript.

Most of all, I remain as grateful now as I was then to my long-suffering 1981 collaborators. The writing was undertaken to a tight deadline dictated by the imminent release of the film *Chariots of Fire* and it was a family effort. My sister, Margaret Magnusson, helped me particularly as interviewer, researcher and critic. My father, Magnus Magnusson, took a delight in checking facts and sub-editing some of the more hastily written passages. At one stage I was creating furiously in one room of the house, while in another room one sister was researching the Olympics and another was typing up my scribbled-over manuscript. In his study, my father was poring over the details of AAA championship records, while my mother was at the kitchen table looking into the Japanese invasion of China. My teenage brother was given the task of hurtling between rooms with the latest gem of research. It was a crazy, unforgettable time – and we made the deadline. Just.

Sally Magnusson,
2007

Introduction

On 17 August 2005, a moving if mildly eccentric ceremony took place in the grimy city of Weifang in eastern China. Sixty years after the ending of the war with Japan and the liberation of Western civilians interned at a camp known then as Weihsien, the Chinese commemorated the occasion with speeches, fireworks and a children's choir. Thousands of youngsters, teachers, residents and city leaders, including Weifang's mayor Zhang Xingqui, turned out at what is now the Number Two Middle School to greet twenty-five former inmates who had travelled there from abroad. At the climax of the ceremony, a fanfare of the *Star Wars* theme tune accompanied the explosion of fireworks into miniature parachutes, representing the American servicemen who jumped from a B-24 bomber to liberate the camp in 1945. This was followed by the release of a flock of pigeons, one for each of the 1,500 Weihsien inmates.

One inmate in particular was honoured. The man near whose grave this ceremony was being held had died a few months before liberation. Eric Liddell was not there on 17 August 1945 to see the paratroopers dropping into the field outside the front gate or to hear the camp band strike up 'Happy Days Are Here Again', but his was the name on the lips of the elderly guests as they exchanged their memories at Weifang. His was the memorial – erected some years previously by Edinburgh University – at which a wreath was laid. It was a formal recognition of the significance the Scots athlete and missionary carries to this day both within China, where the authorities honour his humanitarianism and recognise his symbolic importance to the Beijing Olympics, and across the world, where his extraordinary personal influence has not faded in the eighty years since his Olympic triumph.

Standing at a microphone beside the memorial stone, seventy-eight-year-old Stephen Metcalf, silver-haired and in a smart suit and tie, paid tribute to Eric Liddell, whom he described to the assembled towns-people as a famous Olympic athlete who had given up all to come to China to teach its youth. 'Eric gave me two things,' he told them, recalling the years when he had been one of the 327 children to whom Liddell had devoted himself in the camp. One of these things, he said, was the athlete's own running shoes, repaired with string, which he had handed over to the teenager during the bitterly cold weather of early 1945. 'My own shoes had worn out and it was winter,' said Metcalf, who spent four years in the camp. 'Three weeks later Eric died of a massive brain tumour.'

Yet the best thing Liddell had given him, he told the politely attentive audience, was not shoes but an understanding of forgiveness. 'He taught me to love my enemies, the Japanese,' he said, 'and to pray for them.' He personally had become so inspired by that example that in later years he had given up his job and gone to Japan himself as a teacher, carrying 'Eric's message of true peace'. It was a message he took the opportunity to impress on his hosts at Weifang. 'In these days when China is preparing for the Olympic Games, there are angry protests against the Japanese,' he said. While acknowledging that the Japanese had made a great mistake in trying to sweep their wartime actions in China under the carpet, an attitude he had spent forty years in Japan trying to discourage, he also urged the Chinese to remember the lesson that Eric Liddell had embodied. His was the way of real peace. Metcalf concluded with the emphatic declaration that Liddell had shown 'the best way for athletes the world over to live'.

It is difficult to judge how this somewhat pointed address went down in Weifang that day. China's wartime scars are still angry gashes. But how fascinating that the name of Eric Liddell, already indelibly linked to the 1924 Paris Olympics, was being held up to the hosts of the 2008 Beijing Olympics as an example of how athletes should conduct themselves and how states must come to terms with their past. Quite a legacy for a quiet Scotsman who never believed he was anything special.

The enduring nature of Eric Liddell's influence first struck me in the early eighties, when the forthcoming release of the movie *Chariots of Fire* alerted me to at least the first half of his story. What, I wondered, was so different about this man? Yes, it was true that late in the searingly hot afternoon of Friday 11 July 1924, the twenty-two-year-old science student from Edinburgh University had won a gold medal in the 400 metres at the Olympic Games in Paris. And, yes, it was a memorable race which produced a world record. But there were other people who triumphed spectacularly at those Games: Harold Abrahams of England, who became the first Briton to win the 100 metres; Douglas Lowe, another Englishman, who won the gold in the 800 metres; American Johnny Weissmuller, who took three golds in the swimming; and the incomparable Finn, Paavo Nurmi, who won another four in the track events.

Why, then, was it Eric Liddell who was feted and hero-worshipped for the rest of his life, who had a fan club dedicated to him, a scout patrol named after him, a strip cartoon in his honour in a boys' comic? Why was it Eric Liddell who, nearly forty years after his death at Weihsien, inspired an Oscar-winning film about his part in the Paris Olympics? To these questions must be added now: why should the communist Chinese authorities, hardly known for their affection for Christian missionaries, have been content to see this man honoured with a graveside ceremony in 2005? Why, after so very many years, is his influence among those who still remember him not only undiminished but so remarkably potent?

The answer, I suspect, is not merely because a principle of Liddell's Christian faith led to a refusal to run on a Sunday in the Olympic 100 metres heat, after which he captured imaginations across the globe by unexpectedly winning the 400 metres instead. Rather it lies in the kind of man he was, the unique way he touched lives and lived out his own in the spirit of a passionate Christian faith.

Liddell's sabbatarian gesture appears even more quixotic in these first years of the twenty-first century than it did when *Chariots of Fire* brought his life to the attention of the 1980s. While in 1924 Liddell's actions were widely admired by a society in which Christian observance was still the rule rather than the exception, by 1981 it took David Puttnam's skill as a film-maker and Ian Charleson's charm as an actor to help audiences make the imaginative leap to understanding a man who cared more about honouring the God of the Bible than the deity of sport. In the process, Puttnam detected a new hunger for heroism. But the fascinating twist which his film did not cover is that this very act of principled rejection of potential sporting glory, with plucky success following hot on its heels, was the very thing that turned a modest athlete into a proto-celebrity. After his Olympic triumph, thousands of people flocked to public meetings to hear Eric Liddell speak, schoolgirls swooned in his company and newspaper editorials lauded his example to the young. He became a star.

Perhaps – and here is a further twist – the real renunciation was not his turning down the chance of winning Olympic gold in the 100 metres at all, but having the resolve soon afterwards to abandon the seductions of celebrity and depart for the mission fields of China, where he had spent his early childhood. When he left, just a year after his success at Paris, Scotland's capital gave him the kind of send-off no departing missionary has received before or since. When he died in Japanese captivity, after living away from Britain almost continuously for twenty years, the public reaction was as warm as if he had left the day before.

Although it would be unwise to project the cultural associations of modern celebrity on to a 1920s athlete, there is no doubt that Liddell was a hero of his age who, while content, even eager, to exploit his fame if it meant an opportunity to speak of his faith, yet managed to shrug off the adulation with admirable insouciance when it came to taking up his missionary vocation. What kind of person manages to do that? What kind of person, above all, leaves such a trail of undisputed 'goodness' behind him as he makes his way through life that nobody, as far as I or any biographer has been able to discover, had a bad word to say of him? Most of the people I met while writing this book who remembered him personally are now dead, but every one of them had nothing but praise for him – disconcertingly extravagant praise to a biographer's ears. At the peak of his athletics career, church ministers were writing sermons about his life, comparing him to Christ. When he died, all Scotland mourned. Such a man is heading either for a savage debunking, or else the grudging acknowledgment that he really was, in some quite profound way that had little to do with attributes in which he was markedly lacking, like cleverness or eloquence or overwhelming physical presence, someone special.

But conspicuous goodness tends to bother the sceptical generations which followed his, and it is certainly an inconvenience to a journalist in search of grit. I started out warily. There was surely a pair of clay feet at the base of this pedestal. At the very least there must be some hypocrisy to root out, a streak of spiritual pride, a dollop of sanctimony. 'Oh, come on, was he really that good?' I would ask. The answer was invariably the same, sometimes apologetic, sometimes pained, sometimes indignant, but always the same: Yes, he was.

I thought I was on to something when I happened on a disillusioning eyewitness account of the behaviour of some of the missionaries in the Japanese internment camp. I read of tempers lost and heavy moralising, of exclusiveness and selfishness. The author scarcely had a good word for anyone, least of all for the Protestant Christians. I waited breathlessly for the verdict on Eric Liddell. Then I turned a page and found this: 'It is rare indeed when anyone has the good fortune to meet a saint, but he comes as close to it as anyone I have ever known.' A saint? And this from the scourge of the missionaries.

Speaking to the people who remembered Liddell, I was struck by the delight with which each responded to my invitation to talk about him. I became used to phoning up strangers with an apologetic explanation about writing a book, only to receive an instantaneous stream of warm recollections. Long before I got round to asking, they were anxious to try and put into words Eric Liddell's effect on them. It quickly became apparent that they were not just being sentimental about a departed friend. Somehow, after years and years, his memory still sparkled. I realised that, tricky as it might be to make uncomplicated goodness interesting to read, that was nevertheless my story. My task would be to find ways of communicating the impact of his personality, undeniable to all who knew him yet a little mysterious and difficult to articulate, because, as they all said, he always seemed so ordinary.

Every day's research brought a fresh nugget. The founder of the Eric Liddell Fan Club was a joyous discovery. Still as enthusiastic when I met her twenty-five years ago as she had been as a love-sick teenager nearly sixty years earlier and only a touch less ardent, Elsa Watson evoked a glorious picture of 1920s fan-worship. I treasure her description of residents in her douce block of Edinburgh flats looking out of their windows one morning in 1924 and observing a strange pattern of Virginia stock and nasturtiums sprouting in the garden below. When they looked closely they could make out, bafflingly, the initials E.H.L..

Bob Knight, a retired ship's engineer who had known Liddell in China, insisted in his slow Tyneside way that I rid myself of any notion that his friend was excessively pious. He produced a ribbon of anecdotes to prove it, including one about the time Liddell non-plussed a group of earnest inquirers about the spiritual quality of his running by explaining with a grin: 'I don't like to be beaten.'

Invaluable recollections came from Liddell's sister, Mrs Jenny Somerville, who died in 1994. When I met her in Edinburgh, she was the only surviving member of his childhood family. She was able to tell me about their parents, James and Mary, who started the family tradition of Chinese missionary service. To my astonishment she could remember the tiniest details of life in a Chinese village at the turn of the twentieth century when she was a child.

Annie Buchan, from Peterhead in the north-east of Scotland, was another wonderful discovery: a diminutive, white-haired octogenarian who recalled with amazing clarity the minutiae of life in the Chinese country mission where Liddell worked in the 1930s. Matron of the hospital in the same mission compound, an inmate of the same internment camp, she was at Liddell's bedside when he died and remembered his last words. She told all her stories the same way: simply, clearly, with an eye for details like the colour of the sky and the expression on Liddell's face when he found a dreadfully injured man whose head the Japanese had not quite managed to sever.

Professor Neil Campbell, Liddell's fellow student athlete; Mrs Isobel Herron, the Weihsien schoolgirl who never forgot how Liddell tore up his wife's sheets to mend her hockey stick; Tom Riddell, the veteran sportsman who wished Liddell were around today; General Sir Philip Christison, the officer in charge of the pipe-band of the Cameron Highlanders at the Paris Olympics: there were so many, and their memories not only cast light on Liddell himself, but open a fascinating vista on the social history of the times – on Scotland and China, war and mission, athletics and evangelism.

I left his widow until last. By that time I was so curious, and perhaps a little mesmerised by the charisma that had captivated everyone else, that I approached her with some excitement. You can tell a lot about a man from his choice of partner. And there she was, laughing and vivacious, telling me: 'I can't stand these people who are so goody-goody and holy-holy. They bring out the worst in me and make me want to go the opposite way. Eric was never like that.'

Florence Liddell Hall told me about Liddell's covert but highly inventive style of courtship, his poker-faced sense of humour, his keenly felt hurt at being called a traitor when he refused to run the Olympic heat on a Sunday, his ability to charm exactly what he wanted out of anybody, their home life, their children, the disruptions of living through the Japanese occupation. She told me, too, that Ian Charleson in *Chariots of Fire*, which she had just seen, portrayed her husband exactly as she knew him.

Indeed Ian Charleson, who was to die tragically early himself in 1990, proved another source of enlightenment. I will never forget his description of how difficult it had been to imitate Liddell's style of running – all arms and legs and head thrown wildly back – and then the sudden flash of insight that had shown him why Liddell ran like that: 'He ran with faith. He didn't even look where he was going.'

So what was this faith of Eric Liddell's, so rooted in what some might see as an out-dated religious tradition, yet so potent? What was the source of the serenity everyone talked about and how did he manage to maintain it while being so obviously driven to succeed? What about his charisma as a public speaker, when everyone said he was a poor orator? Was his running really 'an emanation of his well-known spiritual fervour', as one commentator wrote? What was the vein that connected his athletic achievement to his resilience amid the poverty and horrors of war in a primitive Chinese village, and finally to his 'saintliness' amid all kinds of sordidness and privation in the Japanese internment camp where he died in 1945? When I finally looked this man in the eye, as it were, I had a lot of questions.

I also wondered what Eric Liddell would make of modern sport today, and indeed what it would make of him. It is an even more pertinent question now than when I first posed it in 1981. Could he have become an Olympic gold medallist today and still have fulfilled the commitments to his faith and the sharing of it that were so important to him? Would there have been the same joy in running, the same throwing back of the head in the sheer exultation of the race, if he had had to submit to the professional rigours and the extraordinarily exacting standards of sport today? More to the point, could he ever have got away with the quiet announcement of his refusal to run on a Sunday that so impressed his peers, or the uncomplicated decision to slip away from international competition to become a missionary on the other side of the world?

One suspects that after several rounds of the TV studios, a forest of glamourising magazine interviews, an appearance on the list of the world's most eligible men and the planet's cutest bottoms, the enigmatic quality of the man would have been cornered and the unknowable depths that still intrigue people more than sixty years after his death superficially plumbed. And once everything had been aired *ad nauseam*, exclaimed over and explained away, Eric Liddell might have been forgotten.

Instead he was able to leave a mark which the passing of time continues to enhance.

'His Heid's No' Back Yet'

The young man who was carried shoulder-high through the streets of Edinburgh after his graduation, just a week after winning a gold medal at the 1924 Olympics, had a wreath of olive leaves on his head, a wide grin and keen blue eyes. The crowds lining the pavements as he was borne past on a sedan-chair might have noticed, too, that there was not much hair under the wreath. At the age of twenty-two, Eric Liddell's fair hair was already receding, a state of affairs that his disappointed mother ascribed to too many hot showers after training. His build was slight and wiry, and his walk what might be described as springy. The less charitable called it bandy-legged.

In looks, he took after his father, the Revd James Dunlop Liddell, an erect Victorian figure with a long face and luxuriant dark moustache. James Liddell came from the village of Drymen near the southern end of Loch Lomond. He had started his working life as an apprentice in the drapery business in the ancient royal burgh of Stirling, the gateway to the Highlands. But drapery was not to be James Liddell's métier. In the seaside holiday resort of Helensburgh on the coast of the lower Clyde he met the Revd William Blair, a minister of the Scottish Congregational Church, who fired him with a different vocation: to be a missionary in foreign fields.

In 1893, at a Sunday school picnic in Stirling, he met the girl who was to become his wife. Her name was Mary Reddin, a quiet, gentle girl who wore her dark brown hair up in a bun as was the fashion of those days. She had been born in Paxton in Berwickshire, and was working as a trained nurse in Glasgow; she was now convalescing with friends in Stirling after an illness. They were both twenty-two years old and became engaged soon afterwards.

Their marriage was not to take place for another six years, however. James Liddell went on a course at a Congregational college in Glasgow in order to be ordained, while Mary carried on with her nursing. In 1898, he applied to the London Missionary Society and was accepted for a posting to their mission station in Mongolia, in northern China.

Liddell had wanted to get married first and take his bride out with him. But the London Missionary Society was too canny for that. How were they to know if this ex-draper from Drymen would make the grade in the demanding conditions of the field in an alien and even hostile country in the Far East? First he had to go out and prove himself, and pass his exams in Chinese, and only then would they send Mary Reddin out to marry him.

While he was away, Mary took a job in Stornoway, the capital town of the Isle of Lewis in the Outer Hebrides, looking after the fisher girls who flocked to work there during the summer. Stornoway was then the centre of the great west coast herring fishing industry, and the quaysides were alive with activity as the girls plied their sharp knives on the silver catches from more than 300 fishing boats. Accidents were both inevitable and frequent, and Mary Reddin had plenty to do. Her experience of instant first aid in Stornoway was to stand her in good stead later in the paddy-fields of China.

Meanwhile, James Dunlop Liddell was working with a will at learning Chinese, and passed his exams in record time. He was a warm-hearted, peace-loving man who quarrelled with no one and was liked by the Chinese and Europeans alike. The London Missionary Society was delighted with him; his posting was confirmed and after receiving an exultant telegram from her fiancé, Mary Reddin set sail to join him. They married in Shanghai Cathedral on 23 October 1899.

It was not a propitious time for foreigners to get married in China, especially foreign missionaries. China was seething with unrest and resentment against the foreign Great Powers who had humiliated her for decades. The disgraceful Opium Wars in the middle of the nineteenth century, whereby Britain (with armed help from France) forced the Chinese to legalise the import of opium against their will, rankled deeply. China's defeat at the hands of Japan in the Sino-Japanese War of 1894-1895 was fresh and bitter in the memory. Politically, the Great Powers – Britain, France, Germany, Russia and Japan – seemed intent on dismembering China in their greedy pursuit of land concessions, mining rights and ever-increasing trade monopolies.

Under the circumstances, it was not surprising that extreme xenophobia should be flourishing in China at the end of the nineteenth century. When the Liddells married in Shanghai in 1899, this hatred of foreigners was coming to the boil through a secret society called the Yi Ho Chuan, the League of Righteous and Harmonious Fists, better known in the West as the Boxers.

For years the Boxers had been openly calling on the peasantry to join a patriotic militia dedicated to the extermination of all foreigners, especially Christian foreigners. The Boxers were fanatics, which made them all the more alarming; they also harboured the bizarre notion that they were invulnerable to bullets.

In June 1900, the Boxer Rising erupted with a siege of the Western embassy in Peking, now Beijing, and the murder of the German ambassador. The embassies were never captured and two months later the Great Powers sent in an international relief force to lift the siege. Once again, China suffered the humiliation of an imposed treaty: the International Protocol of 1901, which required China to pay huge indemnities and to promise that any Chinese who joined an anti-foreign society, would be summarily executed.

There had been surprisingly few casualties among resident Europeans in Peking, but in the countryside it was a different matter. There it was the foreign missionaries, regarded as agents of Western materialism and promoters of cultural aggression designed to destroy the traditional Chinese way of life, who bore the brunt of the Boxer fury. The Chinese converts to Christianity caught the lash with them.

More than 200 Western missionaries were slaughtered in that uprising, and around 30,000 Chinese Christians are estimated to have perished at the hands of the Boxers. One of the Boxer edicts must have disturbed the sleep of thousands more:

The Catholic and Protestant religions being insolent to the gods and extinguishing sanctity, rendering no obedience to Buddha and enraging Heaven and Earth, the rain clouds no longer visit us; but eight million Spirit soldiers will descend from Heaven and sweep the Empire clean of all foreigners.

It was a potent appeal to superstitious peasants worried about their harvests.

Less than a year after the Liddells were married, a Mrs Atwater of the American Board of Fenchow was writing home:

How am I to write all the horrible details of these days? The dear ones of Shouyang, seven in all, including our lovely girls, were taken prisoner and brought to Taiyuan in irons, and there by the Governor's orders beheaded, together with the Taiyuan friends, thirty-three souls.

The following day the Roman Catholic priests and nuns of Taiyuan were also beheaded, ten souls yesterday. Three weeks after these had perished, our mission at Taku was attacked, and our six friends there, and several brave Christians who stood by them, were beheaded. We are now waiting for our call home.

This was the China into which Eric Liddell was born, a country degraded by foreign intervention and moving inexorably towards revolution. It was in similarly chaotic times that he would die, forty-three years later, as a missionary in an internment camp when China, already in the throes of civil war, was occupied by invaders from Japan.

The Liddells had gone straight to the mission in Mongolia after their Shanghai wedding without even pausing for a honeymoon. Now, with the Boxer Rising convulsing northern China, they had to flee for their lives. Mrs Liddell was pregnant. They had to leave all their belongings except for one small trunk. After a number of alarming adventures they reached the coast safely and took ship to Shanghai. There, in the London Missionary Society compound, Mary Liddell gave birth to their eldest son, Robert Victor. Three months later they again left for the north. Mrs Liddell was installed in the comparative safety of a missionary compound at the port of Tientsin, now Tianjin, to the east of Peking, while her husband made his way back towards their former station in Mongolia to try to find out what had happened to the Christian community there.

Mrs Liddell wrote:

> For four months he was touring Mongolia with Colonel Wei and 200 soldiers, and I could get no word from him. I wish he had written down his experiences. He had a tale to tell that was thrilling, but never attempted to keep a diary. Life was too strenuous and it seemed we must just live a day at a time, as we never knew what would happen next... All winter was a difficult time, murders and horrible things happening.

It was in Tientsin, on 16 January 1902, that their second son, Eric Henry Liddell, was born. The intention had been to christen him Henry Eric, but on the way to church for the baptismal ceremony the order of names was hastily reversed when someone pointed out that the choice of initials, H.E.L., might not be ideal for the son of a Christian missionary.

Baby Eric with his father.

As a result of the Boxer Rising, the mission in Mongolia had been abandoned and James Liddell was sent to a new posting at the village of Siaochang in the province of southern Hopei. Siaochang (known now as Zaoqiang) lay in the Great Plain of northern China, a vast expanse of fields and rivers dotted with little villages. It meant a difficult two-day journey, starting with a six-hour trip by rail south to Techow (now Dezhou) and then a forty-mile trek westwards on a bumpy Chinese cart drawn by two mules. As soon as the infant Eric was old enough to travel, Mrs Liddell took her two boys to join their father in Siaochang.

It is impossible not to be impressed by the casual courage of these missionaries and their wives and children. No journey was too daunting, no accommodation too uncomfortable. When the call came, they went. Siaochang was one of two mission stations in the Great Plain operated by the London Missionary Society. Between them they covered a popula-tion of about 10 million people, living in some 10,000 villages as close to one another, as one traveller put it, as currants in a fruit cake. Every square inch of soil was cultivated, with wheat and millet as the main crops. The climate veered wildly between the extremes of heat and cold, but at least it was mainly dry.

Missionary work had been going on in that vast area for many years, and the nucleus of a strong Chinese Church had begun to emerge with its own evangelists and teachers. The mission station in Siaochang itself consisted of four large houses in a row, with verandas on two sides, both upstairs and down. Behind the houses were the church, a boys' school and a girls' school. The little complex was surrounded by a high mud wall, with a large gate that was closed at night.

Here, in 1903, the Liddells had their third child, a daughter called Jenny, who in later life retained vivid memories of the family's early years in Siaochang. She remembered the devoted Chinese *amah* (nurse) who could not pronounce Eric's name properly and always called him Yellee. The Liddells were the only European children in the compound, and they spent much of their time playing with Chinese children dressed in their padded coats. The men still wore the traditional pigtail, imposed on the Chinese by the Manchu dynasty. Jenny remembered her mother nursing the children through many illnesses, often with no doctor on hand. As a child, Eric once fell very ill with fever, which left him for a long time extremely shaky on his legs; when he was up and about, one lady, as Jenny recalled with a chuckle, was overheard to make the immortal remark, 'That boy will never be able to run again.'

Jenny was an elderly widow in Edinburgh when she shared these memories. She and a younger brother Ernest, born in 1912, stayed in China with their parents until 1929, when ill health forced the Revd James Liddell to return to Scotland for an extended period of rest which turned into permanent retirement. Jenny spent the rest of her life in Edinburgh as the wife of Dr Charles Somerville. She was a charming person to interview, slight and white-haired, soft-spoken and gentle-mannered, with colourful recollections of missionary life in a China which has gone now forever.

For two or three months each year, when the summer heat was at its most unbearable, she and her brothers would escape with their mother to the seaside resort of Pei-tai-ho (Beidaihe), where the mission had built a few cottages on the sea-front as holiday homes. Here they spent the summer months swimming and lazing about, to be joined by Mr Liddell in August when 'his people' were all busy with their harvesting.

In 1907, James Liddell was awarded his first furlough after nine testing years in China, and he returned to Scotland with his family. Eric was five years old; it was the last time he would see Siaochang until he joined his elder brother Rob there in 1937 as a missionary himself.

Mr Liddell took a furnished house for his family in his home village of Drymen, where his father had been an esteemed figure. In *Scotland's Greatest Athlete*, D.P. Thomson cites the memories of a local correspondent:

> Eric's grandfather kept a small grocer's shop in Drymen. He also ran a small wagonette locally known as 'Liddell's machine' to the railway station, about a mile from the village, to pick up any passengers (charge 6d.) or parcels. He was a bearded man, not given to much conversation. He always wore a high bowler hat (never a 'bunnet' like most countrymen), and his white pony ambled along the road at a pace which an active pedestrian could emulate.
>
> The Liddells, a highly respected family, were noted for piety at a time and in a place where evangelism was considered unorthodox. I have a vague recollection of a group of evangelists who used to hold meetings in the village square. I think they belonged to the Faith Mission. The Liddells braved the criticism of their neighbours by coming out boldly in support of these visitors, singing Moody and Sankey hymns.

Since this was the environment in which James Liddell grew up, it is perhaps not surprising that he should have chosen to devote his life to evangelism. This, too, was the family background, with its traditions of personal conviction, against which the two older Liddell boys, Rob and Eric, were to decide to become missionaries themselves.

Rob and Eric started their schooling in the village. But before Mr Liddell returned to China in the autumn of 1908, some more permanent arrangement had to be made, and the boys were sent to the School for the Sons of Missionaries in London which had been founded by the London Missionary Society in 1842. For Rob, aged eight, and Eric, not yet seven, it was the first taste of the family separation inherent in missionary life. The school, which was then at Blackheath, was to move to Nottingham in 1912 and change its name to Eltham College.

Eric made little impression at school to start with. One of his old masters recalled:

> When he first joined us, Eric was very shy, and, physically, rather 'weedy'. He missed his parents greatly, and sheltered as far as possible under his

brother's protection... After two or three years his physique improved rapidly. W. B. Hayward, our headmaster, believed in plenty of fresh air, and two terms of hard 'rugger' per year, with often three, or even four games per week, made of Eric a new man.

It sounds very dated now to call a ten-year-old schoolboy a 'man'; but this was at a time when 'Arnoldism', with its credo that sports were an integral part of the formation of character, was in its heyday. The publication of *Tom Brown's Schooldays* by Thomas Hughes in the 1850s had presented a romanticised view of school games at the immortal Dr Thomas Arnold's Rugby School as an essential contribution to manliness, patriotism, moral character-building, stoicism, courage and team spirit. Dr H.H. Almond, the great nineteenth-century headmaster of Loretto School near Edinburgh, cried out in one of his celebrated sermons:

> Why, oh why, cannot there be a holy alliance between the athlete and the Christian; an alliance against the common enemies of both, against intemperance and indolence, and dissipation, and effeminacy, and aesthetic voluptuousness, and heartless cynicism, and all the unnatural and demoralising elements in our social life?

It was a passionate educational ideal certainly shared by W.B. Hayward, a strong disciplinarian, and by his successor at Eltham College, George Robertson (later headmaster of George Watson's College in Edinburgh). At Eltham it was reinforced by the fact that nearly all the boys came from the same background: missionaries' sons, reared in a family atmosphere of quiet but determined piety. Eltham had its share of 'ragging' and bullying, of course, and Eric Liddell took his full schoolboy share in them; but he is also remembered by a fellow schoolboy for putting a stop to the ragging of a new boy, a frightened and tearful 'man' of seven, when he was being forced to run the gauntlet of a double line of knotted handkerchiefs. Eric was all of eight years old at the time.

At school Eric was popular, though he always seemed a little detached and shy and never had a bosom pal. Academically, he was competent, not brilliant. At sport, however, he shone; he once said to his sister, 'I don't think much of lessons, but I can run.' Not only could he run, but most sports came easily to him; his father had been an excellent gymnast in his day, and his elder brother Rob was also developing into a fine athlete. In fact, the rivalry on the sports field between the two brothers became one of the features of life at Eltham College. The results of the annual school sports day in 1918, when Eric was sixteen and his brother nearly eighteen, make fascinating reading:

Cross Country Run:	1. R.V. Liddell	2. E. H. Liddell
Long Jump:	1. E.H. Liddell	2. R.V. Liddell
High Jump:	1. R.V. Liddell	2. E.H. Liddell
100 Yards:	1. E.H. Liddell	2. R.V. Liddell
	(Equalled school record of 10.8 seconds)	
Hurdle Race:	1. R.V. Liddell	2. E.H. Liddell
Quarter Mile:	1. E.H. Liddell	2. R.V. Liddell

That year, Rob won the Senior Athletic Championship with 27 points to Eric's 23. Eric won it the following year, after Rob had left school, and in the course of it he set a new school record of 10.2 seconds for the 100 yards.

It must be remembered that Eltham College was a relatively small school with only about 150 pupils, which made it fairly easy to shine, particularly during the First World War when so many senior boys left early to go to the trenches. By 1916, Eric was playing cricket in the First XI ('Does not put enough force into his strokes,' commented the *Eltham College Magazine*). By 1918, he was vice-captain ('A good all-round cricketer') and in 1919, at the age of eighteen, he was captain.

Rugby rather than cricket was his real game, though. He was in the First XV by the age of fourteen ('A very light wing threequarter, but has not had much to do; he gets in some useful kicks which would prove better still if there were more strength behind them'). By 1917, he was 'a fast right wing threequarter, who has shown great improvement on last year. Tackling, kicking and falling on the ball are very good. Should do very well next year.' The next year he was captain of the XV at the age of only sixteen:

> He has captained the team with marked success throughout the season, and has been the mainstay of the three line. His kicking is excellent, and his speed and remarkable swerve have decided the issue of several matches. He is the best tackler, and the team is inclined to rely too much on him. He is inclined to be too lenient with the slacker of the team.

The following year he was captain of both cricket and rugby, and a school prefect, too. And yet Eric Liddell was never quite as outstanding

The family. From left to right, back row: Eric, Jenny, Rob. Middle row: Mary (mother), James (father). In front: Ernest.

at school as we might have expected from his popularity and athletic prestige. For instance, he never became head boy, even though he did not leave school until he was nineteen. He never won the Bayard Prize, awarded annually by the vote of his school-fellows to the boy who had exerted the best influence during the year (Rob did, however). Indeed, both the Liddell brothers, talented as they were, had to give best to another outstanding pupil, A. Leslie Gracie, beside whom Eric would later play on the left wing during his fitfully impressive but brief career as a Scottish international rugby threequarter. Leslie Gracie always had the edge on them both. Gracie became head boy. Gracie won the Bayard Prize. Gracie played rugby more dazzlingly than Eric and cricket more effectively. In a trio of athletics champions, Gracie topped the lot by winning every single event on the sports programme on a single afternoon. Yet Eric Liddell the athlete is remembered everywhere, while Leslie Gracie as a sportsman is now a name familiar only to the real aficionados of Scottish rugby football.

Eric left Eltham College in the spring of 1920, needing one subject, French, to complete his entrance qualifications for Edinburgh University, where Rob was already studying medicine. That summer their mother came to Scotland on furlough with their sister Jenny and younger brother Ernest, and they all settled into a furnished house in Edinburgh's Gillespie Crescent.

Eric and Rob, whose lives were to follow a similar course from Eltham College to Edinburgh University to missionary service in China, were much alike – and not just in athletic prowess. Rob was dark-haired and Eric fair, but both brothers were rather quiet and laid-back in comparison to the more exuberant Ernest. Although there was only a year between them, Eric never lost the younger brother's knack of referring anything requiring effort to the senior one. 'Oh, Rob will do it,' he would say cheerfully whenever a task was required.

In their home at Gillespie Crescent, Eric 'crammed' hard and successfully, and in the autumn of 1920 he matriculated at the university for a BSc degree in pure science, a four-year course with combined classes, both practical and theoretical, at Heriot-Watt College (now Heriot-Watt University) and the university itself. He was to prove an able student, especially at inorganic chemistry and mathematics, and was always near or at the top in his class. Even in the Olympics year of 1924, when Eric was training hard on the racetrack as well as studying for his finals, his class-marks never fell below sixty-eight per cent.

*   *   *

Eric Liddell's running career at the university started casually enough. He himself described it in the modest, throwaway style characteristic of the time:

> I had only been in the university a few months before the Athletic Sports came on. Six weeks before this event, a friend, hearing that I had done a little running at school, came round to try to persuade me to enter. I

told him I was too busy. I had a lot of work to get through and no time
for that sort of thing.

In 1921, the Edinburgh University Athletic Club had just formed a
separate Athletics Section, and interest in athletics was running high.
Busy or not, Eric found the time to get in some training, and despite a
six-day cycling tour to the top of Ben Nevis during the Easter vacation
that left his legs stiff and aching, he entered for the University Sports
that May. In the 100 and 220 yards, the favourite was a former Stewart's
College boy, G. Innes Stewart, who was being tipped as a future Scottish
champion. Stewart himself described the two races in a special article in
The Story of Edinburgh University Athletic Club:

> The last Saturday in May arrived, and we were soon trotting out for the
> 100-yards heats. Liddell was on my right, dressed in longish black pants
> and a white vest. Evan Hunter [the starter] got us off to a good start and I
> could see that I was not going to have it all my own way, for Liddell was
> running me very close indeed and I reached the tape only a few inches in
> front of him. In the Final the reverse occurred, Liddell reaching the tape
> an inch or two in front of me. The time was 10.4 seconds.
>
> My self-esteem was to get another rude shock in the furlong, generally
> considered my best distance. Liddell got off to a slightly better start
> and soon gained two yards on me. When we came to the last 80 yards
> I had narrowed the gap to about a yard, and finally got home by a
> matter of inches. The time, 23.4 seconds, was not remarkable, but on a
> slightly uphill grass track with little wind it was probably better than it
> looks.
>
> After that I realised that a new power in Scottish athletics had arrived.

Eric Liddell, the unknown dark-horse freshman, had indeed arrived.
His defeat in the 220-yard furlong was to be the last time he ever lost
a race in Scotland.

His performance that day won him a place in the Edinburgh University
team for the Scottish Inter-University Sports, which meant putting in
some serious training. He was taken to Edinburgh's Powderhall Stadium,
renowned then as now for its greyhound racing. It was the first time he
had run on a cinder track. After that he would go there two or three
times a week for training, practising starts and sprints on one side of the
track to the accompaniment of the barking of excited whippets straining
at the leash on the other.

Training in those days was not the obsessive, all-consuming affair it is today for athletes with high aspirations. Eric Liddell trained regularly but not excessively. The first time he went to Powderhall he felt positively embarrassed at the sight of all the other runners dancing about on their toes as if they were stepping on hot bricks, working their shoulders and bursting into ten-yard dashes. The value of the warm-up was not immediately obvious. For university athletes track-suits were unknown, and on a cold day they would remain in the pavilion until the last possible moment and then emerge, hoping that their overcoats would keep some of the wind from their bare legs below their knee-length shorts.

But Eric quickly learned the vital importance of limbering up properly before a race and slowing down gradually after one. The person who taught him most was Tommy McKerchar, a stocky forty-five-year-old printer by trade, who trained professional runners in his spare time. Spotting Eric at Powderhall one day, he stomped across and introduced himself. According to David McCasland in *Eric Liddell: Pure Gold*, the cigar-smoking McKerchar's opening conversational gambit was a blunt: 'You're too tight', delivered as he dug his fingers into Eric's back. The runner's muscles would snap if they were not softened, he told him, before sending him off for a jog around the track. It was the beginning of a fruitful partnership

Despite his initial embarrassment at the antics required of him, Liddell recognised the need for some training if he was not to end his days a physical wreck. He was grateful for the way in which McKerchar took him under his wing for free and appreciated the brusque discipline which the older man applied to his Powderhall sessions. For the rest of that summer of 1921, McKerchar supervised his training two or three times a week, ending each workout with a thorough massage.

In June, Liddell and Innes Stewart came first and second in the two sprints at the 1921 Inter-Universities Sports, to help give Edinburgh a thumping win over Glasgow, Aberdeen and St Andrews. Soon Eric was winning races all over the country. In the 1922 Annual Sports at Edinburgh University, he won three sprint titles: the 100 yards in a wind-assisted time of 10.2 seconds that equalled the Sports' best performance and the 220 yards (with no wind assistance) in 21.8 seconds, 0.2 seconds under the Scottish Native Record. Even more significantly, he won his first senior 440 yards race (the quarter-mile) in 52.6 seconds.

In the 1922 Scottish Championships he won the 100 and 220 yards, both in good times, and was awarded the Crabbie Cup for 'the most meritorious competitor in the season's Championship'. He was to win it again in 1923, 1924 and 1925 – an unparalleled achievement.

At the 1923 Inter-Universities Sports, he broke three records for the meeting. He won the 100 yards in 10.1 seconds (he had already equalled the Scottish record of 10.0 seconds), and the 220 yards in 21.6 seconds, which was a new Scottish Native Record. His time for the 440 yards, 50.2 seconds, remained an Inter-Universities record until 1957.

In the wake of all this success he was bringing home shelf-loads of trophies. The spoils of the chase were beginning to confound the ingenuity of his mother and sister in finding somewhere to put them all. 'Every week be would bring home prizes,' reported his sister Jenny. 'We were putting them under the bed in case they were stolen.' Among the winnings from that first 1921/22 season for which they had to find room in their new home in Merchiston Place were, not counting all the cups, a silver rose bowl, a cheese and biscuit dish, a three-tier cake stand, a large clock, a silver tea-set on a tray, a kettle, fish servers, silver brushes and combs, six tea fish-knives and forks, another six tea-knives, a flower vase, a leather suitcase, a travelling clock, a silver entree dish, a case of cutlery and a crop of watches. No one in the Liddell family would ever go short of a gold watch.

Contrary to the impression given by the film *Chariots of Fire*, there was never any opposition from the family to his athletics. 'We were all thrilled to bits about his running,' said Jenny, who felt a little hurt at being portrayed in the film as a prim character who tried to encourage Eric to concentrate more on his religion. 'I was a naïve, unsophisticated teenager at the time. I would never have dreamed of telling Eric what to do.'

Eric was meanwhile notching up rugby successes to add to his athletic triumphs. In his second year at university he was playing for the First XV at centre threequarter, impressing everyone with his blazing speed and determination. Within a couple of months, in his first season of playing senior rugby, he was featuring in the international trials, playing on the left wing outside his former schoolboy partner, Leslie Gracie, who had matured into a centre threequarter of devastating pace and elusiveness. In the two trials, Liddell scored no fewer than ten tries. *The Scotsman* commented magisterially on the first game: 'This game will long be remembered by those present for the brilliant combination which A.L. Gracie and E.H. Liddell made... The pair give promise of being the fastest wing Scotland ever had.' After the second trial, *The Scotsman* was even more effusive about Eric Liddell:

His great speed is not his only asset; for not only did he 'round' one, and sometimes two, opponents when he scored, but time and again he had to use both resource and initiative. Never once was he found wanting. He showed an almost uncanny intuition for being in the right place at the right time, and no matter how unconventional Gracie might be in some of his offensive tactics, Liddell refused to be taken by surprise, as quite excusably he might have been. He has learned the use of the reverse pass, and in defence he is improving with every game he plays.

After the trials, the selection of the 'Gracie–Liddell wing' was a virtual certainty. In the next two seasons, they were to play seven times together for Scotland, during which Scotland lost only once (the 1923 Calcutta Cup match against England at Inverleith Place, Edinburgh), before Eric retired from rugby to concentrate on athletics. It was a record that any internationalist would be proud of: seven games, only one lost. Yet there is something perplexing and oddly inconsistent about his career as an international rugby player, something missing somewhere, as with his career at school. Despite his tremendous speed, despite his courage in the tackle and his celebrated swerve, his game seldom really 'came off'. *The Scotsman* vacillated between praise and faint praise. Against Ireland in 1922: 'That he is a great player in the making there is no doubt, but there were times when he showed a rawness in his work and lack of resource when cornered.' Against France in 1923: 'The Gracie–Liddell wing was as meteoric and mercurial as ever; Liddell was the more efficient of the two, and seemed to be putting more fire in his play than is his wont.' Against Wales at the Arms Park, Cardiff, in 1923:

> Gracie was the vital, living force in the threequarter line. His partner on the wing, E.H. Liddell, improves every game he plays. He runs now with more determination than he showed last year, and he showed real grit and some football on several occasions. Had he a less extraordinary man beside him, he might be much more dangerous than he is ever allowed to be.

This was the occasion of one of Scotland's most famous victories over Wales in Cardiff, by 11-8. It was Scotland's first win there since 1890, and after the game was over, the Scottish threequarters were carried shoulder-high off the field by their sporting Welsh opponents.

In Liddell's last international, the Calcutta Cup game with England, there was more than just the disappointment of defeat: 'The Scottish threequarter line was not seen to advantage. Nothing can be urged against Liddell. He got few chances, and, although hardly so prominent as against Ireland, he ran with fine resolution.'

Like many a 'speed-merchant' in rugby, Liddell has sometimes been thought of as simply a sprinter rather than a footballer. Yet paradoxically he loved rugby more than any of the other sports he enjoyed. The sporting journalist William A. Reid summed it up shrewdly:

> Liddell liked running, but he loved football. For all that, he was not a natural footballer, as he was a natural runner, and although he was too plucky and too good a tackler to be stigmatised as a 'mere sprinter', he had not the attributes, the knack, and the craft of the great football player.

With the merest hint of sisterly bias, Jenny Somerville puts it this way: 'Eric, unfortunately, got a reputation, so there was always somebody to spot him and mark him. So he never got the chance he might have had if he had not been marked so closely. Anyway, he gave up rugger because he started concentrating on his running.'

Yet amongst all the rugby, the running and the studying, something even more important was happening in Eric Liddell's life. It came to a head on the day his friend and future biographer, the Revd Dr D.P. Thomson, invited him to speak at a Christian evangelistic meeting in Armadale, an industrial town in West Lothian in the central belt of Scotland. The meeting was to be part of a vigorous campaign in central Scotland that was being run by the Glasgow Students' Evangelistic Union, which had been founded the year before. Thomson was deputed to ask Eric Liddell, already the best-known athlete in Scotland, to come and address a special meeting for men in the Town Hall. His brother Rob was already involved in this interdenominational student crusade, and it was believed that Eric himself was even now contemplating the possibility of work overseas. D.P. hitch-hiked to Edinburgh on a lorry and went straight to the Edinburgh Medical Mission Hostel at 56 George Square, where Eric and Rob were now lodging after their family's return to China. Thomson put the proposition to him directly. Eric dropped his head for a moment to consider it, and then said, 'All right. I'll come.'

That meeting at Armadale was a watershed in Eric Liddell's life, because it was the first public confession of the Christian faith which was to inform the rest of his life so vividly. Until then it had been a private matter. At school he had been a regular member of the weekly Bible class, where attendance was wholly voluntary, but he had never taken part in any of the discussions. In due time he had become a full communicant

Eric Liddell.

member of the Church at the age of fifteen, helped to form a branch of the Crusaders' Union at the school and assisted in the work of the Islington Medical Mission. His faith had always been firm but unspoken. It seems to have been real to him virtually from childhood, taught by his parents and accepted by their children. Eric had found his own answer to the universe at an age long before most people realise there is a question, and he never saw any reason to doubt it.

No one ever talks of Eric Liddell expressing doubts. He never seemed to be exercised by the nagging intellectual questions that so often ruffle the serenity of the modern believer. His widow, Florence, said he never spoke of doubts, although he might have had them. He read voraciously and often felt discouraged, but doubts? On the whole she thought not: 'It was a simple, personal faith.' Was this naivety? Or was it rather an intellectual innocence which apprehends truth with a child-like clarity that eludes the worldly-wise? It is difficult to tell with a man like Eric Liddell. He was so much the product of a particular missionary family and a particular religious tradition; yet he was to invest that inheritance with an awesomely distinctive character that transcended the stereotype.

His faith was rooted deep in the evangelical tradition, which accepts the Bible not just as a collection of wise maxims and cautionary tales but as the embodiment of the truth about mankind, man's destiny and his relationship with God. The principle of keeping the seventh day of the week holy as a day of rest, which was soon to hurl Eric Liddell into international prominence, sprang from these beliefs. Principles like that had been instilled into him from boyhood and his nature was not that of the restless questioner. He listened, he accepted, and then, like the perfectionist he always was, he worked on it until his faith was so deeply ingrained in his personality that he came to live his life in a way which people, reminiscing over his incandescent memory, would over and over again call Christ-like.

That first public evangelical meeting at Armadale on 6 April 1923 was the beginning of a life of dedicated service to God. There were only some seventy or eighty men present, but they listened attentively. In the evangelical campaigns that followed, culminating in his year of public speaking after the 1924 Olympics, people came flocking to listen to him. Of course the press had something to do with that, for Eric Liddell was the Scottish superstar of the 1920s, a celebrity who could always attract an audience. Yet his fame alone hardly explains his attraction, especially in view of his diffidence as a speaker. Since he spoke quietly and sometimes rather monotonously, his huge audiences were not being mesmerised by oratory. Even his most fervent admirers never claimed that he had a particular way with words.

Indeed Eric himself was keenly aware of his own inadequacy in putting across his convictions to large groups of people. After the release of *Chariots of Fire* in 1981, his widow told producer David Puttnam that one of the reasons she loved the film was that his 'wee man' (actor Ian Charleson) had done something which Eric could never have done for himself. 'When your wee man opens his mouth,' she told Puttnam, 'it's Eric, but it's Eric able to talk in a way Eric never could.'

This makes it all the more remarkable that, wherever Eric Liddell went, whether in Scotland or later in China, he could command such rapt attention. It seems to have been the genuine power of his personality that drew people, the compulsion of his belief, the down-to-earth quality of his sincerity. People were aware of a strength they could never quite put a finger on. Eric Liddell talked without rhetoric about ordinary things: what he had done that day, what he felt about this and that. He told them that Jesus could make a difference to the way they lived their lives tomorrow. He told them that the Kingdom of Heaven was God living inside them, and that this was where the power to have faith came from, and the power to run a race well.

In everything, he had the common touch, the ability to talk to anyone like a friend and make that person feel both important and challenged. That must be why no one who recalls even the most fleeting contact with Eric Liddell has anything less than the most fulsome tribute to pay him. Whether it was a Chinese coolie, an Olympic Games masseur, a Glasgow down-and-out, a Japanese soldier, a schoolgirl with a crush, a hospital matron, a nagging colleague, they were all treated to the same approach: a smile, a kind word, a self-deprecating joke to put them at their ease.

Eric's behaviour at athletic meetings is a case in point. Those who remembered him from those days rarely talked of his running without adding something about the kind of man he was. Innes Stewart, his first major opponent at the University Sports in 1921, wrote: 'He was very modest, rather shy, and most pleasant to talk to.'

Neil Campbell, later professor of chemistry at Edinburgh University, was a fellow-member of the Athletic Club and used to race against Eric. He recalled that on one occasion Eric offered to exchange the places they had drawn for the 440 yards. Neil Campbell was drawn in the outside lane, and in those days there was no 'stagger' to the lanes at domestic meetings; everyone had to make a mad scramble for the inside of the track after the gun. Eric, knowing that he was the more experienced of the two, was happy to give his fellow-competitor the advantage of the inside track. Professor Campbell wrote: 'No athlete has ever made a bigger impact on people all over the world, and the description of him as "the most famous, the most popular and best-loved athlete Scotland has ever produced" is no exaggeration.'

The stories of Eric Liddell from this time are full of tales of his chivalry on the racetrack. It is difficult to tell them without making him sound insufferably well-meaning, although this does not seem to have been how the gestures came across to fellow-competitors. Once he went up to speak to a black runner whom no one else was speaking to, and engaged him in conversation. Invariably he would offer his opponents the trowel he used to dig holes for starting, and then shake hands with them all before the race. No one seems to have wished that 'Liddell and that damn trowel of his' would go away. His chivalry seems to have been accepted as naturally as it was offered.

By this time, the 1924 Olympic Games were approaching, and specu-
lation was mounting as to which sprinters would represent Great Britain.
As late as June 1923, Eric Liddell had not been seen on a running track in
London, and the short-distance times he had been recording in Scotland
were still inconsistent enough to make his Olympic selection a matter
of some doubt. But his performance at the AAA Championships at
Stamford Bridge in London that July changed all that. He won the 220
yards in 21.6 seconds and the 100 yards in a new British record of 9.7
seconds. That record would not be broken for thirty-five years (Peter
Radford in 1958 in 9.6 seconds), which makes it one of the longest-
standing records in British athletics.

If that was not enough to clinch his selection for the British Olympics
team, then his performance at Stoke-on-Trent the following week certainly was. That was the weekend that Eric, representing Scotland in the
Triangular Contest with England and Ireland, won all three sprints: the
100, the 220 and the 440 yards. That triple win was in itself a unique
achievement; but it was his astonishing performance in the 440 yards
which has gone down in the annals of athletics.

There he was, three strides into the race, when suddenly he was stum-
bling on to the grass. J.J. Gillies of England, bursting through for the inside
berth, had knocked Eric off the track. For a moment he hesitated, thinking
he was disqualified. But a number of officials signalled him urgently to
continue and spectators watched, mesmerised, as he sprang forward again
and went pounding after his opponents. By now they were twenty yards
ahead of him. Surely he could never make up that kind of distance?

Arms swinging, fists punching the air, head thrown back, he began to
draw on the leaders. He was fourth now, ten yards behind Gillies. Forty
yards from home, he was still only third and on the point of collapse.
But with another superhuman effort, incredibly, he was there. He was
first. He had beaten Gillies by two yards and his time was 51.2 seconds.
He had given a top-class field a start of twenty yards – worth a full two
seconds – and won. At the tape he collapsed in exhaustion. It was one of
the great races of all time, and the crowd rose to him as he was carried
from the field. As *The Scotsman* said next day:

> The circumstances in which he won it made it a performance bordering
> on the miraculous. Veterans whose memories take them back thirty-five
> years, and in some cases even longer, in the history of athletics, were
> unanimous in the opinion that Liddell's win in the quarter-mile was the
> greatest track performance they had ever seen.

He ran that day, everyone said, like a man inspired. Yet modern coaches would have been aghast at his running style. His old opponent, Innes Stewart, put it politely: 'Liddell had a curious action, swinging his arms very high, bringing his knees well up, and throwing his head well back.'

In fact, his arms seemed to attack the air, clawing and punching. His chin was up, his head so far back that he seemed at times to be gazing at the sky. He wobbled a bit as he ran, too. But that extraordinary style propelled him towards the finishing tape faster than anyone else in the world. And the exhilaration on his face as he ran, the exultation as he threw back his head, were never to be forgotten. People were always entranced by their first sight of Eric Liddell running at full tilt.

His old running companion, Professor Emeritus Neil Campbell, found Liddell's unorthodox style thrilling. 'His style has, in my opinion erroneously, been described as ungainly,' he wrote in an Edinburgh University journal in 1992:

> He certainly ran with a style all his own, which perhaps lacked the grace and flow of such great runners as Milkha Singh, whose running impressed so many of us at the 1958 Commonwealth Games, but he ran with a thrilling rhythmic power and drive which brought spectators to their feet. To quote a *Scotsman* reporter: 'Liddell was a magnificent sight in full flight.'

A fascinating insight into the way Liddell ran came from Ian Charleson, the actor who played Eric Liddell in *Chariots of Fire*. 'Liddell's style was a problem,' he said:

> I had to learn to run properly and then to learn Liddell's way. The hardest thing was that Eric ran with his head back, but when I did it I couldn't see where I was going. I kept running off the track and bumping into other runners.
>
> Then one day, on the fifth or sixth day of filming, I suddenly cottoned on to what he must have been doing when he ran. At drama school we used to do what are called 'trust exercises', where you run as hard as you can towards a wall and trust someone will stop you, or you fall off a piano and trust someone will catch you.
>
> I suddenly realised that Liddell must have run like that. He must have run with his head up and literally trusted to get there. He ran with faith. He didn't even look where he was going. So I can see how that would have given him a lot of extra push in a way. He just let go, completely relaxed.

That moment when he threw his head back, opened his mouth and set his chin seems to have been the moment that Eric Liddell found something extra. At an athletics championship at Hampden Park in Glasgow, a spectator once remarked to the bowler-hatted Glaswegian next to him that Liddell would be hard put to it to win this race. It was the last lap of the 4 x 440 yards relay and Liddell had forty yards to make up.

'His heid's no' back yet', was the laconic reply. Whereupon, as the spectator reported later, back went the head and Liddell left his opponents standing to win by twenty yards.

Where he got that extra push from when his head went back is anyone's guess. His sister told the story that when someone asked him the secret of his success at 440 yards, he said: 'The first half I run as fast as I can, and the second half I run faster with God's help.' But just as typical is the reply quoted by Bob Knight, a former ship's engineer from Tyneside who used to call in on Eric years later when his ship docked in China. Bob was with Eric when someone was introduced to the famous athlete and commented on how frequently he had looked as if he was going to lose a race and then suddenly came away with a burst of speed. The guest, and the assembled company, waited for Eric to tell them how he had put up a prayer or called on the Lord, but according to Bob Knight, there was no such pious reply. 'He smiled that quiet smile of his,' said Knight, 'I can see him now. And he said, "The fact is, I don't like to be beaten."'

That is also what Eric told his running mates the day they were out jogging and a corporation bus drew alongside and hooted a challenge. No one but Eric had the energy for that last, uphill spurt. He raced after the bus and beat it to the top of the hill. 'I don't like to be beaten,' he explained when the others caught him up.

No, Eric Liddell did not like to be beaten. He wanted to be the best. From the moment the starting gun went off, he was out to win. That explains the set of his teeth, the determination to stretch his body to the limits, the sheer grit that hurled him to the finishing line against sometimes insuperable odds. But it doesn't invalidate Ian Charleson's discovery that he ran, in a sense, by faith. D.P. Thomson insisted that in the three months after the public confession of his faith at Armadale, Liddell ran more brilliantly and achieved greater distinction as a sprinter than ever before. It may indeed be that there was a connection. Liddell didn't like to be beaten, but he also exulted in running for its own sake, with mind, body and soul in it together. So if his spirit was in a sense liberated in those exhilarating months, it is perhaps small wonder that he threw his head back and found new resources of strength in his legs and lungs as well.

Whether he could have been the same runner today under the constraints of modern sport is something else. His diet would certainly have appalled a modern coach. Eric was living with twelve or thirteen others in the Edinburgh Medical Mission, so he just ate what they were given. He tried to avoid too much heavy food on the day of a race, but that was not always possible. 'On one day on which I ran, I took plum pudding,' he said later, 'and that day I ran the second fastest "quarter" I have ever run in Scotland.'

Whatever he ate before a race, Eric was now a certainty for the 1924 Olympics in Paris. He would run in the 100-metre sprint, at which he had always excelled and was reigning British Champion, and the 200 metres. The 100 metres was the jewel of the Games and Eric wanted to win it.

Then the timetables came out. The 100-metre heats were on a Sunday.

2

'I'm Not Running on a Sunday'

'I'm not running,' he said, and nothing would budge him. He didn't make a fuss, but he was absolutely firm about it. The Sabbath was God's day, and he would not run. Not even in the Olympic Games.

The British athletics authorities were horrified. It was early in 1924, only a few months before the Eighth Olympics in Paris, and Eric Liddell was Britain's main hope for the 100 metres. He was their golden boy. And now he was saying he would not run in the qualifying heats of the 100 metres because they were being held on a Sunday. It was tantamount to throwing away a gold medal for Britain.

Eric made his decision known as soon as the timetables for the Olympics were announced. 'It was all very quiet,' said his fellow student athlete Neil Campbell:

> Liddell was the last person to make a song and dance about that sort of thing. He just said, 'I'm not running on a Sunday', and that was that. And he would have been very upset if anything much had been made of it at the time. We thought it was completely in character, and a lot of the athletes were quietly impressed by it. They felt that here was a man who was prepared to stand for what he thought was right, without interfering with anyone else, and without being dogmatic. Quietly, he just said, 'I'm not running on a Sunday.'

Jenny Somerville, Eric's sister, did not think it was a tortuously difficult decision for him to make at the time. The Olympics were still some months ahead and not, as popular legend has it, on the morrow. Neither was it a dramatic, last-minute change of mind, as some sports writers have suggested. Eric Liddell and the sporting authorities had known for a long time that he could not, and would not, compete in the 100 metres if the heats were to be run on a Sunday.

Reverence for the Sabbath was as natural to Eric Liddell as breathing, and infinitely more precious than a gold medal. It probably did not even occur to him to try to rationalise it. Or did he have doubts? Did he try to persuade himself that he would be honouring God as much by winning a race for Him as by having a Sabbath rest? Did he ever wonder if it would not be a finer thing to sacrifice his principles just this once for the sake of a gold medal for his country? If these thoughts ever occurred to Eric Liddell, he did not voice them, or let them stay long. Indeed, it is unlikely that he was ever persuaded that national honour on the sports field counted for very much at all. Memories of the grotesque national follies which had convulsed the world in the 1914-1918 war were still too fresh. After his eventual triumph in Paris, he told Captain Philip Christison of the Cameron Highlanders, who had organised an impromptu Scottish air from his piper to give Liddell 'a lift' at the beginning of his race, that he had not been running for Scotland. As Christison described it in a BBC documentary in 1984, Liddell told him: 'We've had enough of struggles between nations. The Olympics are not a struggle between nations and should never be like that. The Olympics are individual events to find out who is the best in his particular event and I was running for myself to prove I was the best.'

Although his stance was understood and accepted by many of his countrymen, when the announcement was made some felt he was letting his country down. He had to contend with public jibes and press criticism, which hurt him. His wife Florence, to whom he told the story many years later, was in no doubt that he felt the criticism. 'He was called a traitor to his country, and I think he felt it quite keenly,' she said.

His friend Greville Young, who was sharing a student hostel with him in Edinburgh's George Square, said it caused 'a tremendous furore', particularly in the newspapers. In scenes anticipating the alarming treatment of newsworthy individuals today, the press descended on George Square. Greville Young said:

> They hammered on the door demanding to see him. And on one occasion it was my job to go down and try and clear them off. It was quite menacing. And there were cries of 'He's a traitor to his country.'
>
> But Eric just accepted these things. I never remember him being upset. He said, 'It's just my belief. I don't criticise others about it, but I'm not going to run on the Sunday.'

Although the newspapers gave him a hard time, Eric had the support of many athletes, one of whom was so impressed by Eric's stand that he actually followed his example at another race meeting some time after the Olympics. The man was Tom Riddell, eight times Scottish champion miler between 1925 and 1935. He used to run in medley relay races with Eric, with Riddell on the half-mile leg and Liddell on the quarter-mile. He described Eric as 'a terrific influence on all of us athletes at the time', so much so that when Tom Riddell was chosen to run in a race-meeting in Italy and learned that the race was to be run on a Sunday morning, he withdrew. 'That was because of Eric's example,' he said. 'Without the slightest doubt, Eric Liddell was the greatest athlete Scotland has ever produced, by his influence, his example and his capabilities.'

Eric had also declined to run in the Olympic 4 x 100 and the 4 x 400-metre relays, for which he had been selected; their heats, too, were to be run on a Sunday. But it was his refusal to run in the 100 metres that was the real blow to the athletic authorities. Only the previous year he had established himself as one of the fastest men in the world, when he won the AAA sprint double in 9.7 seconds for the 100 yards and 21.6 seconds for the 220. His time for the 100 yards had been only a tenth of a second short of the world record, and no British sprinter would excel it for another thirty-five years. It was little wonder that he had been hailed as the man who could capture the Olympic 100 metres crown for Britain for the first time since the revival of the Games in 1896.

With Eric Liddell's withdrawal, British hopes now switched to Harold Abrahams, a talented student who had been notching up steadily improving times for Cambridge University and in national contests. But no one, least of all Abrahams himself, was unduly optimistic about his Olympic chances. There would be a formidable team of American sprinters in Paris, with a flush of superior times among them. Abrahams had a 9.9-second 100-yard time to his credit – equivalent to between 10.7 and 10.8 seconds for the 100 metres. But Charles Paddock of the United States, the reigning Olympic champion, had been unofficially credited with 10.2 for the slightly longer 110 yards. So Abrahams had little cause to feel confident.

Harold Abrahams, born in 1899, was the son of a Lithuanian Jew. His was an exceptionally athletic family: his elder brother Sidney won the AAA long-jump title in 1913. Harold's own running debut was at the age of ten at Stamford Bridge, London, then the mecca of British athletics. In 1918, as a pupil at Repton, he began to make a name for himself by winning both the 100 yards and the long jump at the Public Schools

Championships. During a short spell of army service in 1919, he raced against his boyhood hero, the legendary sprinter Willie Applegarth, who had won a bronze in the 200 metres at the Stockholm Olympics of 1912; Lieutenant Abrahams was given a start of two yards on the twenty-nine-year-old champion and beat him by six yards in 10.0 seconds. Later that year, Abrahams went up to Cambridge to study law at Caius College, and launched himself on a dazzling student athletics career. Between 1920 and 1923 he won an unprecedented eight out of nine events in the annual athletics contests with Oxford; in his final appearance in the 'Battle of the Blues', he won the 100 yards in 10.0 seconds, the 440 yards in a career best of 50.8 seconds and the long jump with an English Native Record of 23ft 7¼ins.

Abrahams later claimed that much of the passionate zeal he put into his running was fired by the anti-Semitism he encountered at Cambridge. Caius College strongly refutes the allegations of anti-Semitism in the 1920s and was so piqued by the elaboration of this theme in *Chariots of Fire* that it declined to cooperate with the shooting of the Cambridge scenes. This uneasy relationship between Abrahams (who died in 1978) and his *alma mater* makes an interesting contrast with that of Eric Liddell and Edinburgh University, who not only feted their favourite graduand in 1924 but honoured his memory fulsomely with a gala performance of *Chariots of Fire* in the spring of 1981 and a memorial stone which they despatched to China to mark his grave in 1991.

During the winter of 1923/24, Abrahams trained hard with an eye to the Olympics. Four years previously he had been selected for the Antwerp Olympics while still a freshman at Cambridge, only to be eliminated in the second round of the 100-metre heats. This time he was determined to do much better; and who better to help him do that than Sam Mussabini, the coach who had already trained those fine Polytechnic Harriers sprinters, Willie Applegarth and Harry Edward (winner of the Olympic bronze medal for the 200 metres at Antwerp in 1920). Three times a week Harold Abrahams trained under Sam Mussabini's severe eye, paying a meticulous attention to the mechanics of running that was far ahead of its time.

He recalled later:

Sam was 'dead nuts' – that was the expression he used – on the arm action, with the arms kept low, bent at the elbows (we used running corks for a good grip): he maintained, which I believe to be absolutely sound, that the action of the arms very largely controls the poise of the body and action of the legs. My training sessions consisted largely of perfecting the start and practising arm action over and over again. There were no starting blocks in those days, and we took meticulous care with the placing and digging of holes and the accurate control of the first few strides. I always carried a piece of string the length of the first stride, and marked the spot on the track, at which I gazed intently on the word 'set'.

Our partnership was ideal, because Sam was not an autocrat. We discussed theory for many hours and argued and argued until I accepted that his theories were sound – not because of his experience and knowledge, but because my mind was satisfied with his reasons. We paid infinite attention to my length of stride multiplied by the rapidity with which a stride is taken. I used to put down pieces of paper on the track at measured distances and endeavour to pick them up with my spikes as I ran. I shall always believe that the vital factor in my running in Paris was that by conscientious training I had managed to shorten my stride an inch or two and get an extra stride into my 100 metres. Then Sam encouraged me to work on a 'drop' finish [the dipping lunge at the end of a race to get your chest to the tape first in a tight finish].

The contrast with Liddell is irresistible. His arm action alone would have driven Mussabini 'dead nuts'. Nevertheless, the differences should not be overplayed. Harold Abrahams himself was quick to defend Liddell's running action. 'People may shout their heads off about his appalling style,' he commented once. 'Well, let them. He gets there.' It is also true that Liddell worked harder at his running than many of his friends realised and, although Tommy McKerchar was no Sam Mussabini and confined himself mainly to practising starts and pummelling muscles, he injected a discipline into their afternoons at Powderhall that Eric's insouciance somewhat masked.

But although neither Liddell's commitment nor Abrahams' inner fire should be underestimated, it is still easy to see why these two men made such a neatly balanced pair of protagonists for the film producer David Puttnam. He was surely right to sense that specialised coaching was the key to Abrahams' success at Paris, while the secret of Eric Liddell's triumph was in some inscrutable way a matter of the spirit. Whatever it was that could lift the Scotsman to his astonishing feats of athletic achievement, it had little to do with counting strides.

Liddell and Abrahams had not raced against each other, although they had been expected to meet in the AAA championships at Stamford Bridge in 1923. But Abrahams, suffering from a septic throat that day, failed to reach the final. Liddell did reach it. That was the day he won the 100 yards in 9.7 seconds and became Britain's great hope for the Olympics. But now Liddell was out of the Olympic 100-metre sprint. The problem was what on earth to do with him. In the end he was asked to train instead for the 400 metres in Paris. And that was how Eric Liddell discovered that he was a natural quarter-miler.

Of course, his amazing recovery and victory in the Triangular Contest race at Stoke-on-Trent in 1923 had shown he could run the 440 yards if he felt like it. But he had never trained seriously for it; it had never been thought of as 'his race'. Conventional sporting wisdom considered that the 100 and the 200 metres went together in an athlete's training, as did the 400 and the 800. So perhaps the man who would come to be hailed as the world's finest quarter-miler might never have fulfilled his potential if an insuperable obstacle in the shape of his conscience had not overturned all the traditionally accepted ideas about it, and turned the 400 from a middle-distance race into a sprint.

As his wife Florence recalled:

> Eric always said that the great thing for him was that when he stood by his principles and refused to run in the 100 metres, he found that the 400 metres was really his race. He said he would never have known that otherwise. He would never have dreamed of trying the 400 at the Olympics.

The quarter-mile, or the 400 metres (there is a difference of only about two metres between them), is one of the most demanding races of all. A more recent British Olympian, Adrian Metcalfe, has described it as:

> a sprint which also possesses those features one admires most in middle-distance events: stamina, the need to fight till the tape, the virtual masochism of pleasure through prolonged pain – a race in which one's body reaches to one's internal conflict. Physically the race is simple. But to make oneself do it... that is the challenge which, if overcome, yields the tremendous satisfaction.

It has always been a glamour event in which the unexpected has become almost expected. More than fifty years earlier, in 1868, a brilliant runner called Edward Colbeck had won the quarter-mile at the English Championships under the most bizarre circumstances. Halfway through the race, which was being run on the Beaufort House field in

West London, a sheep wandered on to the track. Colbeck crashed into it, breaking the poor creature's leg and losing some eight yards (about a second in time). Yet he clocked up 50.4 seconds, his best ever run. It would be nearly twenty years before the runner broke the magic 50-second mark, winning the AAA title in 1886 with 49.8 seconds, an achievement as notable in its time as Roger Bannister's breaking of the four-minute barrier in the mile at Oxford in 1954.

The 400 metres had not been a particular British speciality in the early Olympics. In the very first Olympics at Athens in 1896, Britain's second string, Gilbert Jordan, had won the silver, close behind the American winner, Thomas Burke. In the fourth Olympics, the London-born Scot Lieutenant Wyndham Halswelle of the Highland Light Infantry won the gold medal at the newly opened White City Stadium in the saddest of circumstances. In the final, which he was contesting as favourite against three Americans, J.C. Carpenter of the USA was disqualified for bumping and boring in the home straight. When a rerun was ordered, the other Americans boycotted the race in protest and Halswelle was left to run the distance solo to win the gold medal in a time of 50.0 seconds, well below his previous best of 48.4.

By Eric Liddell's day, the 400 metres (or 440 yards, as it was usually run in Britain) was becoming a British preserve – or at least an Olympic event for which British hopes could reasonably stand high. In the Olympic year of 1920, two student runners at Oxford and Cambridge, Guy Butler and the South African Rhodes scholar Bevil Rudd, were vying for world supremacy after dead-heating in the annual Oxford *v.* Cambridge match in 49.6 seconds. In the Olympics themselves, on a rain-sodden track at Antwerp, Rudd snatched the gold, again in 49.6 against Butler, who was closing on him fast. That silver medal was the first of four Olympic medals that Butler would win in his outstanding career.

In 1924, British hopes once again rested with Guy Butler; Liddell was not rated as anything more than an outsider. Unfortunately, Butler suffered continuously from a 'game' leg which seriously handicapped his career as a runner; when the Olympics came round, his thigh was heavily bandaged and he had to start from an upright position instead of using the faster crouching start.

Eric Liddell trained vigorously in the few months left to him before the big race. His blood was up now, but he had a long way to go. No one understood the challenge he faced in the 400 metres better than Tommy McKerchar, who was able to give strategic advice on the running of a race which required careful pacing to achieve the distance without sprinting to early exhaustion. But hard though they worked in their two or three times a week training sessions at Powderhall or Craiglockart in Edinburgh, it was clear to both that this was an uphill struggle. As David McCasland has aptly put it in *Eric Liddell: Pure Gold*: 'Down at Cambridge, Sam Mussabini convinced Harold Abrahams that he could find him an extra two yards in the 100. McKerchar would have to find an extra three hundred yards for the Flying Scotsman.'

At the AAA Championships, held within a few weeks of the Olympics, Liddell fended off British, Canadian and American opposition to win in the respectable time of 49.6 seconds. But as the Games drew near, his chances of beating the cluster of Olympic entrants, all of whom were credited with times around 48 seconds, looked extremely remote.

The Paris Games, which opened on Saturday 5 July 1924 to a crowd of about 60,000 people, ushered in a new era in the Olympic movement. It is true that if you watch the archive film footage you are struck by how small everything looks compared to the mammoth occasions staged in modern times. You also notice the relative sparsity of spectators in the stadium, even in the audience-drawing events like the major races. Yet in reality these Games were bigger than any preceding them. There were forty-four nations competing this time, fifteen more than at Antwerp, and more than 3,000 participants, some 500 more than last time. Only ten years previously the world had ripped itself apart in the first of the century's terrible wars and the wounds were still angry: it would be another four years before Germany was invited to send a team to the Olympics. But the mood in Paris was cheerful and celebratory, with a panache which gave these 1924 Olympics an incipiently modern feel. With a contingent of 400, the Americans brought particular flair to the occasion. They arrived in a liner and a battleship with a flamboyant retinue of trainers, coaches, masseurs, managers and a chaplain.

It was also a memorable year for sporting achievement. In track and field events, six world records would be set that year and fifteen Olympic records equalled or surpassed. The swimmers set two world records and equalled or beat ten previous Olympic marks; one of their stars was the great Johnny Weissmuller, who won three gold medals (and another two in 1928) and went on to make his name and fortune as the screen Tarzan.

The Olympic motto, *Citius, altius, fortius* (Faster, higher, stronger) was coined for these Games by a sports-loving French schoolmaster. Huts appeared for the first time around the stadium: not exactly an Olympic village, but at least a step in the direction of collective accommodation.

Women competed in fencing for the first time; and lawn tennis and rugby football saw their last Olympics.

But what everyone would remember the 1924 Olympics for, above all, was the searing heat. Never before had the Games been staged in the temperatures in which the Colombes Stadium sweltered that month of July. A cauldron, some called the stadium. Others described it as a furnace. One of the refreshment stalls was pointedly dubbed La Bonne Frite (The Good Fry). On some days the temperature soared as high as 45°C. Runners in the 10,000 metres cross-country race were dropping like flies; only twenty-three of the thirty-eight starters finished the course.

The 2nd King's Own Cameron Highlanders were stationed in Cologne at the time, and were sent to Paris as the official British musicians for the Olympics. Their first duty was to lead the march of the British athletes up the Champs-Elysees to lay a wreath at the tomb of the Unknown Warrior. HRH Edward, Prince of Wales, laid the wreath, and four pipers played that infinitely poignant lament 'The Flowers of the Forest', which mourns the calamitous Scottish defeat at the Battle of Flodden in 1513.

Captain Philip Christison was in charge that day. In the front row of the party of British athletes he noticed his fellow Scot, Eric Liddell, someone he was to see a good deal more of that week, because they were both staying at the Hotel du Louvre. Captain Christison had the task of getting Liddell and the other British athletes to the stadium in time for their events. Despite the innovation of huts near the stadium, many of the athletes were still scattered in hotels all over the city. The Americans complicated the process by carrying their competitive spirit on to the streets and monopolising the taxis at higher fares than anyone else would offer. The harassed British captain had to resort to stopping private cars in the street and pleading with the drivers to get the athletes to the race in time.

Liddell and the captain met from time to time in the hotel lounge for a chat, and Eric confided to him that his decision not to run in the 100-metre heat still weighed heavily on his mind.

'I wonder if I'm doing the right thing?' he would say. But he always added a minute later, 'No, I'm sure I'm right.' The captain, later to become General Sir Philip Christison, recalled that Eric was still under pressure from his teammates to run the 100 metres. There was no acrimony in it, but Eric was made to feel keenly that he was letting king and country down. Although Liddell had reservations about whether national honour had any place in the Olympics at all, coming so soon after the First World War, he nevertheless knew it was rare for a Scot to reach this class in athletics and he was not allowed to forget that his behaviour was considered 'less than cricket'.

Lord Cadogan, who was among the numerous British dignitaries at the Games, had given the team a little pep-talk at the start. 'To play the game is the only thing in life that matters,' he told them. Whether or not his words were an implicit rebuke to Liddell, *The Scotsman* heaped its own coals of fire when it reported them the next day. 'There is not the least doubt,' said the paper, 'that the British team will play up and play the game, thus upholding the honour and reputation of Great Britain.'

On the day when he should have been on the sprint track doing what Lord Cadogan considered the only thing in life that mattered, Eric Liddell was preaching at a Scots church in another part of Paris. *Chariots of Fire* has him preaching on a text from the Old Testament prophet Isaiah, whose commentary in chapter 40 on man's vain bid to 'go it alone' is made to resound around the little church while the athletes are seen pounding the track on the other side of the city.

'Hast thou not known, hast thou not heard,' cries the screen Eric Liddell, 'that the everlasting God, the Lord, the Creator of the ends of the earth, fainteth not, neither is weary?... He giveth power to the faint: and to them that have no might he increaseth strength. Even the youths shall faint and be weary, and the young men shall utterly fall.' His voice rises. 'But they that wait upon the Lord shall renew their strength; they shall mount up with wings as eagles; they shall run, and not be weary; and they shall walk, and not faint.'

There is not a scrap of evidence that the real-life Eric Liddell actually preached anything of the kind, or that he would have carried it off with anything like the flair of Ian Charleson. But he must have known the passage well, and he would no doubt have loved to quote it back at Lord Cadogan. Indeed, life actually copied art in a most satisfying way in 1991 when part of that quotation was chosen for the inscription on a memorial stone near his grave in Weifang, the Chinese authorities blissfully ignorant of the religious significance of the words.

On the following day, Monday 7 July, Liddell was back in the Stade Colombes to cheer Harold Abrahams on to victory in the semi-final and then the final of the 100 metres. Abrahams settled his feet in the starting-holes (starting-blocks were not patented until 1927), with the words echoing in his mind that Sam Mussabini had written to him in a note just before the Games opened: 'Only think of two things – the report of the pistol and the tape. When you hear the one, just run like hell till you break the other.' Abrahams did just that, and burst through the tape with his celebrated drop-finish at 10.6 seconds, with Jackson Scholz of the USA less than a metre behind, and Arthur Porritt of New Zealand winning the bronze.

Abrahams was the first European to win this, the most coveted of sprinting honours, and remained the only British athlete to have won it until Allan Wells of Scotland carried it off in 10.25 seconds at the Moscow Olympics in 1980 (these Games were disrupted by a US-led boycott and his time was outside the Olympic and world record of 9.95 seconds). Abrahams said later that he owed it all to Mussabini. 'Under his guidance I managed to improve that decisive one per cent which made all the difference between supreme success and obscurity.'

The following year Abrahams seriously injured his leg while long-jumping and never competed again. But he often remarked on the difference the Olympic medal had made to his life. It gave him the impetus to break into journalism and broadcasting at an early age, and guaranteed him universal respect as he began to climb the administrative ladder of sport. While Liddell was teaching Chinese school-children and diffidently refusing to speak of his Olympic triumph, Abrahams was being appointed to ever higher athletics boards and honestly welcoming the potency of gold. He died in January 1978, a leading and esteemed figure in the athletics world.

On Tuesday 8 July, Liddell cruised through the heats of the 200 metres. Abrahams and William Nichol of Great Britain were also through. On the same day, Douglas Lowe won the 800 metres for Britain in just half a second outside record time.

Wednesday 9 July saw Liddell and Abrahams lined up together with four Americans for the final of the 200 metres. It was won by Jackson Scholz in a record 21.6 seconds, with Charles Paddock second. *The Scotsman* informed its readers the next day that Abrahams had been sixth and last. Halfway through its description of just how Abrahams had gone about being last ('running like a selling plater', as Abrahams was later to say), it casually offered the additional information that 'Eric Liddell, the Scottish sprinter, scored points for Britain by running into third place'. Noting that Liddell failed to produce his strong finish, it added: 'He was well placed and had his spurt been forthcoming he would undoubtedly have won.' The fact that Liddell had won a bronze medal for Britain at his first Olympic appearance, and that he was the first Scot ever to win an Olympic medal in the 200 metres, was not brought to the readers' attention.

Nothing illustrates better than this low-key press coverage the immeasurably different status of the Olympic Games then and now. A country so recently at war had other priorities than medal tallies. Even when *The Scotsman* announced to the Scottish public two days later that they now had an Olympic world-record quarter-mile champion, the information came three quarters of the way down its news summary:

'E. H. Liddell, the Edinburgh University sprinter, set up a world's record for the 400 metres at the Olympic Games,' it declared sedately, directing attention to page nine for a full report. On page nine we find 'Olympic Games, Liddell's Great Victory' sandwiched between 'Nature Notes, Young Hedgehogs and the Cannibal' and 'Liberal Policy, Opponents' Handicaps'. The report itself, though, is lengthy and full of colour.

Similarly, on 8 July the press reported that Mr Ramsay MacDonald was leaving for Paris for talks with the French Premier. Two days later he had returned to London. Yet no one had linked the Prime Minister's name with the Stade Colombes and the Games or thought fit to comment on the fact that he had been to Paris and had not, even unofficially, visited the stadium for a few minutes to cheer on his compatriots.

On Thursday 10 July, Liddell cruised through his first-round heat of the 400 metres in the mediocre time of 50.2 seconds, well behind the winner. Later that day he won his quarter-final in a personal best of 49.0. Next day he won his semi-final in 48.2. Liddell was clearly coming into top form at exactly the right moment. His time, however, was slower than that of the American Horatio Fitch, who had just shattered the world and Olympic record in the other semi-final in 47.8 seconds, and slower than the Swiss runner Joseph Imbach, not to mention the gallant Guy Butler who had qualified for the final in a European and UK record of 48.0. There was little to suggest, that Friday afternoon, that Liddell would take world athletics by storm later the same evening.

On the morning of that momentous day, Friday 11 July, Eric had been handed a note. But the one he received was rather different in tone from the message Sam Mussabini had sent to Harold Abrahams, urging him to think of nothing but the pistol and the tape, and run like hell. Liddell's note was rather more quixotic, and much better material for legend. It read: 'In the old book it says, "He that honours me I will honour." Wishing you the best of success always.' It was signed by the athletics masseur who attended to Eric and the rest of the British team. The biblical reference was to 1 Samuel 2, verse 30: 'Them that honour me, I will honour.' He wrote it, as he revealed later, simply because he 'liked Eric so much'.

Eric accepted the note at the Hotel Moderne in the Rue de la República and said he would read it when he reached the stadium. Lying on the treatment table in the dressing room after the race, he thanked the masseur for the note. 'I did his left side,' the masseur, a man with a romantic bent, recalled later, 'and I remember what a great heart he had.'

The Stade Colombes was still baking hot when the six competitors gathered on the track for the 400 metres final that evening. There were two Britons (Liddell and Butler), two Americans (Horatio Fitch and Conrad Taylor), a Swiss (Joseph Imbach) and a Canadian (David Johnson). Liddell went round shaking hands with all his opponents before the start as usual. As his loquacious masseur commented, he must have been saying goodbye to them because they wouldn't be seeing him again – he would be so far in front. That sounds like hindsight: Liddell had been drawn in the dreaded outside lane, the worst possible place for a relative novice at the event, where he would have to set the pace on his own without knowing how his opponents were faring.

Suddenly, with a blast of pipes and a swirl of kilts, the improbable strains of 'Scotland the Brave' filled the stadium. Only fifty yards from the starting line-up, the pipers of the Cameron Highlanders had sprung into patriotic action. With a fellow Scot in the final of the 400 metres, the temptation had proved irresistible to their young captain. 'Oh, we just wanted to give Liddell a lift,' said General Sir Philip Christison. 'The atmosphere was so light-hearted that I said, "Come on, let's strike up", and there was nothing the French could do to stop us.'

His aide was a piper by the name of Corporal Thompson. In 1990, at the age of ninety-nine, Christison told Radio Tweed in an interview from his home in Melrose, 'When the time came for Eric Liddell's race, I said to him, "Look here, Thompson. As soon as he gets on to the starting blocks, you blow up Scotland the Brave." And he did. Of course the French rushed to try and stop him but it was too late.'

After the race, Eric thanked Captain Christison for the gesture, although he added: 'But I don't think it put an extra yard on me.' He said he had not been running for Scotland but for himself, to prove he was the best. It was then that he spoke of the Olympic Games not being a struggle between nations, but between individuals. The next day he joked to a reporter from the London *Evening Standard* that he suspected either the army general or the British team captain of a dark plot to terrify the opposition.

Pipe-Corporal Thompson managed a full, mischievous eight bars before the race began. At last the stirring strains of the pipes died away. The six finalists settled in their marks and tensed. The pistol cracked, and Eric Liddell in the outside lane was off like a greyhound. People long remembered with awe the blistering pace he set in the first half of that incredible race. He flashed past the 200-metre mark at 22.2 seconds – only 0.6 of a second slower than Scholz's winning time in the 200 metres final two days earlier. He was now some three metres clear of his nearest rival, the bandaged Guy Butler, who was making a tremendous effort on the inside.

There was no possibility of Liddell keeping it up, the aficionados were thinking in the stands: no one could sprint the first 200 metres of a 400-metre race flat out, and stay the pace to the end. He was bound to 'blow up' in the home straight, if not earlier. Besides, that energy-wasting style of his, the antithesis of a streamlined action, could surely never hold out.

As the runners came off the bend into the straight (there was only one bend at the Stade Colombes because the track was 500 metres, which meant the 400-metre track wasn't a full circuit), Fitch was beginning to make up ground. He had overtaken Guy Butler (who would win the bronze) and was now chasing hard after Liddell, who was only two metres ahead of him.

And then the incredible happened. At the moment when another runner might have started to flag, however determined, Eric Liddell somehow summoned up hidden reserves of strength and stamina. Head back, chin forward, mouth open, knees jumping, arms waving, he put on a spurt and started to increase his lead over Fitch. At the tape, he was all of five metres ahead, and had won the Olympic title in a record time of 47.6 seconds.

To anyone who knows anything about running, that sensational race was, and remains, almost unbelievable. The time has been bettered, of course, in the inexorable advance of development and technique: the current Olympic record for the 400 metres is 43.49 seconds, set by the American sprinter Michael Johnson at Atlanta in 1996, and the current world record is Johnson's eye-watering 43.18 at the World Championships in Spain in 1999. But it wasn't really the time that mattered; it was the way in which the race had been run, and won.

To give *The Scotsman* its due, its report on the inside pages was unrestrained:

1924 Olympic Games: Liddell winning the 400 metres.

The Union Jack flew in proud majesty over the Colombes Stadium today for the only final down for decision, the 400 metres, which resulted in a great victory for Great Britain. The brilliant running of E.H. Liddell, the Edinburgh University sprinter, was responsible.

There was a gasp of astonishment when Eric Liddell, one of the most popular athletes at Colombes, was seen to be a clear three yards ahead of the field at the half distance. Nearing the tape Fitch and Butler strained every nerve and muscle to overtake him, but could make absolutely no impression on the inspired Scot. With twenty yards to go, Fitch seemed to gain a fraction, but Liddell appeared to sense the American, and with his head back and chin thrust out in his usual style, he flashed past the tape to gain what was probably the greatest victory of the meeting. Certainly there has not been a more popular win. The crowd went into a frenzy of enthusiasm, which was renewed when the loud-speaker announced that once again the world's record had gone by the board.

The Edinburgh *Evening News* was even more ebullient:

> All round the banked area, people were on their feet cheering madly,
> and as if by magic, hosts of Union Jacks appeared above the heads of the
> raving crowd as Liddell ripped through the tape and into the arms of the
> Britishers who were waiting for him. For a moment the cheering lasted,
> then from the loudspeaker came: 'Hello, hello. Winner of the 400 metres:
> Liddell of Great Britain. The time 47⅗ is a new world's record.' Again
> the great roar of cheering went up, and there were long minutes before
> the announcer could convey that Fitch, of America, was second, and
> that Butler, who ran second in this event to Rudd, the South African, at
> Antwerp, was third and Johnson, of Canada, fourth. Thrill followed thrill,
> for the flags went up, a big Union Jack in the centre, a little one to the
> left, and a little Stars and Stripes to the right, and again came that hush
> as all the spectators stood and the bands played. Then came crash upon
> crash of applause as Liddell walked across the grass and vanished down
> the stairs to the dressing rooms.

Liddell's time of 47.6 seconds was officially ratified as a world record for
the 400 metres. It was not the fastest time in the world, however; the
great American runner, Ted Meredith, had earlier recorded 47.4 for the
440 yards, which is more than two metres longer. But after watching
the race from the stands, Meredith had nothing but praise for Liddell.
He told a reporter that it was the most wonderful quarter-mile that had
ever been run. Considering the conditions under which it was run, it
was nothing short of marvellous, as Liddell had had to make his own
pace from the crack of the pistol to the tape. 'Liddell,' said Meredith, 'is
the greatest quarter-miler ever seen.'

Watching footage of that sensational race today it is striking how calm
Liddell looked afterwards. After crossing the finishing line he stands
there quite composed, smiling comfortably, with no outward appearance of either exhaustion or jubilation. He just looks hugely content.
He has done it. He has proved he is the best. And he has done it the
right way.

Immediately afterwards, all sorts of people rushed into print to
announce that Liddell was a natural quarter-miler and they had always
known it. Newspapers which had once called him a traitor now lauded
him to the skies, casting off their bland reportage for the occasion. The
colour-writers had a field day, as in the Edinburgh *Evening News* feature
report:

It was Liddell who first caught the eye as they came round the first bend. The Scot set up a terrific pace. He ran as if he were wild with inspiration, like some demon. And as he flew along to the accompaniment of a roar, the experts wondered whether Liddell would crack, such was the pace he set out to travel. 'Liddell' was shrieked, 'Imbach' was thundered by the Swiss, 'Taylor' was shouted by a finely drilled American clique; 'Butler', 'Fitch' in turn were yelled. Liddell, yards ahead, came round the bend for the straight, and as he did so he pulled the harder at himself, for Fitch was getting nearer. There was Butler too, and Imbach to be reckoned with. It was the last fifty metres that meant the making or breaking of Liddell. Just for a second it was feared that he would kill himself by the terrible speed he had got up, but to the joy of the British camp, he remained chock full of fight. Imbach, perhaps fifty yards from the tape, fell. It was then Liddell or Fitch. The Scotsman had so surely got all his teeth into the race that the American could not hold, and Liddell got home first by what, considering the formidable opposition, was almost a remarkable finish. Butler was third, Johnson next, and then Taylor, who had the bad luck to stumble a yard or two from the finish.

The *Bulletin*, Scotland's popular picture-paper of the day, called Liddell's race 'the greatest achievement in the Olympic Games so far', and went on:

> This is the crowning distinction of Liddell's great career on the track, and no more modest or unaffected world champion could be desired. Liddell has built up his success by hard work and perseverance, and although hardly a beautiful runner he has even triumphed over his defects of style.

These 'defects of style' made his win all the more remarkable. 'That lad Liddell's a hell of an awful runner,' Jack Moakley, wisest and oldest of the American team, had remarked the evening before the race, 'but he's got something. I think he's got what it takes.' Nobody could quite define that something, and the last person to try was Liddell himself, who was content to tell an interviewer afterwards that he had just 'gone all out'.

Liddell did not stay in the stadium for long after his race. He had an address to deliver on Sunday at a church service in the old Scots Kirk in Paris for all the Olympic competitors, and he slipped away quietly to prepare it. Behind him, pencils scribbled and wires buzzed and the race was relived on a thousand tongues. Already they were speculating: would he have won the race he never entered, the 100 metres? It has been asked many times since, and it remains the great unknowable.

But fifty-six years and twelve Olympics later, somebody else, in a fanciful sort of way, ran the 100 metres race for him. A Scotsman won the jewel of the sprint titles at last. And when Allan Wells was asked after his Moscow triumph in 1980 if he had run it for Harold Abrahams, the British winner from 1924, Wells replied quietly: 'No, this one was for Eric Liddell.'

3

'This Awful Grim Business'

Of course, Eric Liddell would hardly have recognised the kind of Olympic Games that Allan Wells attended in 1980, hyped by an excitable media and disfigured by international politics, far less the twenty-four-hour global sensation it had become by the time Athens hosted the most recent Games in 2004. 'This awful grim business that passes under the name of sport', is how Laurie Liddell, former Director of Physical Education at Edinburgh University, described modern sport.

These days television cameras rove the stadium, picking out the gigantic electronic scoreboard, the perfect curves and synthetic surface of the running-track, the vast armies of officials and journalists and photographers and security police; the artfully placed names of commercial sponsors. Athletes spring past, decked from head to toe in the sporting equipment necessary to run a perfect race: lightweight running-vest and pants, specially spiked shoes, track suits, windcheaters. Their bodies are taut, minds concentrated on releasing the fruits of months of training into one magnificent explosion of speed or height or endurance; calves moulded and muscled from mile upon mile of road and track foot-pounding; thighs bulging from agonising sessions of press-ups and weight training.

In the commentators' boxes, staffed by battalions of broadcasters, the talk is of form and training and drug-tests and the costs and rewards of ambition; the language is the rhetoric of heartbreak and tragedy, joy and sacrifice. It reflects a world where sport is god, a universe away from a place where you dug your own starting holes with a trowel, modestly shook hands with your opponents before a race and confined yourself after victory to the comment that you merely 'went all out' to win Olympic gold.

Willie Carmichael, a vice-president of the SAAA and former Commonwealth Games organiser, roared with laughter at the thought of what Eric Liddell would make of sport today. He picked up a picture of Liddell posing with some running mates and stabbed it gleefully with his finger: 'Look at his long pants and short sleeves. Nobody wears that today. And look at him in this picture. He's standing there in his blazer, freezing. British athletes just didn't have tracksuits in those days, or anything fancy like that.'

However, the relatively minor question of attire would not be the only problem to confront Eric Liddell. His attitudes, his expectations, in fact his whole way of life would have to undergo a revolution. And, according to Tom Riddell, the former Scottish champion miler who ran with Eric in the old days, he would not have appreciated many of the aspects of the modern style:

> Eric would turn in his grave if he saw the way today's athletes run around with the name of commercial advertisers emblazoned on all their gear. He'd have been appalled at the sight of 'amateurs' running for money. And as for those fellows who do a lap of honour after winning a race...

Professor Neil Campbell, who ran against Liddell at Edinburgh University in the twenties, thought that even with all the opportunities that the sophisticated techniques of sport today have to offer, Eric would probably not have been prepared to take advantage of them:

> If he was around today he'd still have been a splendid runner, but I don't think he'd have been able to participate in all the big championships here, there and everywhere. I just don't think he would have done it. Training in those days wasn't like now. A seven-day-week training session was just not on for him with his studies and other commitments. His training was fairly intensive, but only two or three times a week. There was nothing like the fantastic dedication of today. Although he wasn't a particularly great student Eric's studies were all-important to him. He got a great deal of pleasure out of running, but it took second place.

The kind of dedication which puts sport in only second place is just not good enough today if you want to be a top athlete. The insights we had at Athens in 2004 into the cost of success at Olympic level were instructive. British marathon runner Paula Radcliffe's emotional trauma as her body simply refused to perform under the unforgiving Greek sun when it mattered most was painful to watch. She sat at the side of the road with her head in her hands, four years of inexpressible effort lost as the race she was expected to win went on without her. For once the commentators' hyperbole seemed appropriate: this really was despair. Then in the days that followed we witnessed the exact opposite: Britain's ex-army runner Kelly Holmes incoherent with delight at becoming a double gold medallist in the 800 and 1500 metres. Her unaffected ecstasy was heart-warming and infectious, but even here was something faintly alarming about how intensely it all mattered, especially when she admitted afterwards that the years of not making it to the top had nearly destroyed her.

In her autobiography *Black, White and Gold*, rushed into print months later amid the whirlwind of publicity which followed her Athens success, Kelly Holmes (by then Dame Kelly) wrote of reaching a point where she felt she could not take any more injuries and pain. Crying uncontrollably, she had picked up a pair of nail scissors and started to cut her left arm with one of the blades, one slash for every day that she had been injured:

> With each one I felt I was punishing myself, but at the same time I felt a sense of release that drove me to do it again… After that, whenever I felt low, I'd excuse myself and go to the bathroom where I would break down again and get out the scissors to mark yet another day of injury.

Holmes added: 'I don't pretend to understand what I was doing, and I definitely knew it wasn't right, but I couldn't help myself. I had reached a place that I couldn't get out of.'

That difficult stage passed and eventually the dream Kelly Holmes had pursued single-mindedly since the age of fourteen was realised, twice, at the podium in Athens, when she became only the third woman in the world to achieve the middle-distance double. As she wrote of her 1,500 metre triumph: 'It had taken years of dedication, commitment, focus, emotional struggle and pain but now I had done it. I was double Olympic champion, with a new British record of 3:57:90.'

Was it worth it? Kelly Holmes certainly believes it was. Olympic victory fulfilled her deepest desire and, in the modern way of things, utterly transformed her life. But the cost over the previous twenty years was high – and as many athletes know, there is sometimes no end to the wait, no consummation of the desire or ultimate payback for the sacrifices.

The intensity of modern training is not a new development. Forty years ago, the 400 metres hurdler David Hemery was undertaking a gruelling non-stop sixty-week build-up for the 1968 Olympics at Mexico

City, where he won the final by the huge margin of seven metres and lopped seven tenths of a second off the previous world record. It might even be argued that Harold Abrahams, who is thought to have been the first British athlete to have a personal coach in Sam Mussabini, was right in there at the beginning of this trend.

If given the chance now, Eric Liddell might well have been glad of the benefits that modern training has to offer. He was far too much of a competitor not to be intrigued by the opportunities that today's sporting techniques offer the athlete of running even faster. But he would undoubtedly have been discouraged by how comprehensively the pursuit of athletic excellence consumes the life of the athlete.

As Ron Pickering, sports commentator, coach and former athlete, put it:

> In Eric Liddell's time, training was not so exacting that he couldn't think of higher things, academically and spiritually; whereas now if athletes are planning to enter the ministry they wait until later in their career. No athlete today could go and train two or three times a week and get away with it; in Liddell's day, it was merely par for the course. The demands of training mean that athletes now have to change their lifestyle and ration their time. If, for example, an athlete wants to go to university, then he'll have to take four, five, even six years to do a three or four-year course. It's damn difficult, if you are a coal-miner, to be an athlete today, and impossible to be a swimmer or a gymnast. It's difficult to contemplate the world's greatest miler wanting to be a surgeon today, but that's what Roger Bannister had his sights set on.

So Eric Liddell would have had to choose between a career in sport and a career as a missionary, and that would have been no choice at all in Liddell's eyes. He might also have decided that sport today is just too serious a business to be worth the candle. Eric ran to win, but he also ran because he enjoyed it. Laurie Liddell (no relation) believes the joy has gone out of high-level sport today:

> It has ceased to be play; it's just jolly hard work to stay at the top in modern sport. I wonder occasionally if we're getting our priorities a little wrong. I really think we're getting to the stage now where we've got to ask where the demarcation line is between what used to be this lovely, enjoyable activity that we all could take part in, and this awful, grim business that now passes under the name of sport.

It's a cry from the heart of so many former athletes and trainers from Liddell's time. One senses a despondency for the future of sport, a yearning for the good old days of dedicated amateurism. But the nostalgic glow which clings to those times may obscure the way sport was already developing and changing by the time Eric Liddell was electrifying the athletics world. Indeed the progress of the modern Olympics from the first Games in Athens in 1896 shows a steady increase in innovation, professionalism, size and seriousness.

In 1896, only thirteen nations were represented and only nine sports were on the programme: cycling, fencing, gymnastics, lawn tennis, shooting, swimming, track and field athletics, weight-lifting and wrestling. Those Games were so informal that a British lawn tennis player entered the Olympic tournament simply in order to secure a court to play on, because the courts were in the Olympic stadium. And several of the 500 entries were inquisitive tourists visiting Athens for the first time and eager to share in all the new experiences on offer. By the time of the Third Olympics at St Louis in 1904, there were twenty-five competitions. A suspiciously fresh-looking marathon runner called Fred Lorz won the race by fifteen minutes, but was disqualified when it was revealed that he had hitched a lift for ten miles of the course in a truck.

The 1912 Games in Stockholm saw an important development when Sweden, the host nation, became the first country to employ a professional coach to prepare its Olympic team. Within two years, Britain and Germany had their own national coaches, but the First World War meant there were no Berlin Games in 1916 at which the athletes could show off the fruits of their professional preparation. This sort of professional coaching was then abandoned until the next Berlin Games in 1936.

By the Paris Olympics of 1924, the Games were no longer recognisable as the cosy occasion launched by the Hellenic Olympic Committee in Athens on Easter Sunday, 1896. In those days, the 311 athletes who attended all came to Athens on their own initiative and at their own expense. By 1924, there were already subsidised national teams, a form of sponsored nationalism. Almost from the outset the Olympic Games were moving away from the vision of the original idealists.

For many years the Games were attended by only a tiny minority of the world's nations and athletes. The Third World hardly got a look-in, while the huge but socially backward nations of Russia and China had too many problems to be concerned with a mere athletics competition. The United States and western Europe dominated the Games, and even then only a fraction of the populations of these countries had the opportunity to compete. In the 1924 Olympics, almost twenty per cent of the British team were Oxbridge students.

At a time when women in many parts of the Western world were struggling for social and political rights, it is not surprising to learn that the Olympics were all-male affairs for the first thirty years of their existence. The breakthrough came in 1928 when women were allowed entry into the Amsterdam Games. The programme was admittedly somewhat modest, with only five events; but a start had been made, and world records were produced at each of the events. However, the women's cause suffered a setback when the 800 metres was dropped from the Olympic calendar because of the distress shown by several of the finalists. It was not reinstated in the women's programme until 1960.

The pace of innovation speeded up after the Second World War. At Helsinki in 1952, the USSR entered the Games for the first time and began to show its formidable potential, with its team performing well in the men's events and dominating the women's events. Training underwent radical changes. As the sports writer Tom McNab points out in *The Complete Book of Athletics*, more was discovered about athletics techniques and training methods in the years between 1952 and 1960 than had been unearthed in the previous 2,000 years.

Technology was also changing the nature of athletics. Until 1964, cinder or clay tracks were used at the Olympics and other major championships. But by the time of the Mexico Games in 1968 the Tartan track, a synthetic resin surface patented in the USA and originally designed for horse racing had been generally accepted as the best all-round track for performance in all weathers and ease of maintenance. Starting-blocks, invented in 1927, came into general use after the Second World War, so that a trowel was no longer an essential part of an athlete's sports equipment. Since 1964, the official timing of competitors at the Olympics has been provided by photo-finish devices.

Other developments were not regarded as being quite so healthy for sport. After the 1960 Games became the first to be shown on televisions around the world, the increasing demand for televised sport transformed athletics in the West. Television inevitably attracted sponsors, and sponsorship money, along with state aid and sports scholarships, increasingly created athletes who were amateur only in name. It was a development much lamented by those who valued the sporting ideals epitomised by Eric Liddell's generation.

On the other hand, it is worth remembering that the Ancient Greek athletes were not amateurs either. They were fully supported during

training and often well rewarded afterwards. The concept of amateurism was actually a device introduced by the Victorians to prevent the
working classes from competing against the aristocracy, who could afford
the luxury of training without the inconvenience of having to earn a
living. For a long time, sustaining the romance of amateurism required
athletes to have private means or to try to fit training around a job. It
took until 1988 for the situation to be finally clarified. After the Seoul
Olympics, all professional athletes were declared eligible for the Olympics,
subject to the approval of the international federations in charge of
each sport.

The trend which has caused the greatest concern is the use of
performance-enhancing drugs by athletes. Not that this has been an
entirely modern phenomenon. As early as the 1904 Olympics, the runner
Thomas Hicks was given multiple doses of strychnine and brandy in the
course of the marathon, which he not surprisingly won. And in 1920
the American victor in the 100 metres benefited from a concoction of
sherry and raw egg, which was administered by the national coach just
before his race. Full-scale drug-testing began in 1972 and at Olympic
level is now very reliable. Most sports administer doping tests to at least
the medallists in each event. Since 1966, it has also been found necessary to require women at major international competitions to undergo
a sex-determination test.

Drugs, sex tests, money, media hype and two hours of urgent con-
sumption of drinks after every winning race in order to produce a urine
sample... there is much that Eric Liddell would find bewildering, and not
perhaps hugely impressive, about modern sport. But perhaps the sports
world would not be particularly impressed with him either, in a professional sense. Tom McNab, a British National Athletics coach from 1963
to 1977, has argued that despite remarkable race times for the amount
of training he did, Liddell would be unlikely to win an Olympic title
nowadays. 'You see, Eric was only five feet nine inches. He would be
limited by his size. And his potential would definitely have been in the
100 metres, not the 400.'

McNab studied how Eric Liddell ran in great detail. A winner himself
in 1952 of the Eric Liddell Memorial Cup for the best junior athlete in
Scotland, he was responsible for teaching the *Chariots of Fire* actors how
to run. As he said: 'I had to teach Ian Charleson how to run, and then
I had to train him how to run badly.' Although he described Liddell
as 'God in action', he insisted that his achievements should be put in
perspective.

'In those days very few people ran. They usually went to university, which meant that the majority of them were from middle-class backgrounds.' He recalled that even thirty years later, when Clydesider Jimmy Reid heard the news that Roger Bannister had broken the four-minute mile in 1954, he held up a pair of spiked running shoes and asked the men in the dockyards how many of them owned a pair themselves. No one put up a hand.

No, Eric Liddell was very much a man of his times, and it is ultimately fruitless to transpose him to a world in which conditions and opportunities are so different. 'Sport was very much a recreation in those days,' says Tom McNab:

> And Eric Liddell reflected that attitude. What he was doing then was much more cavalier, much more fun than the attitude today. The fun is still there, at the bottom level, where more and more people have the chance to enjoy themselves. It's at the top that it's a lot less fun. The training is hard and there's a lot of pressure. But it's like the difference between going to the theatre and seeing a farce or a Shakespearian tragedy: the farce is fun, the tragedy isn't, but they both give immense pleasure.

McNab is a realist. He regrets some of the unhealthy influences in sport today, but is too aware of the advantages that progress has brought to want to turn the clock back. 'Professionalism is here to stay. It's just a matter of admitting it.'

Others fear that excessive professionalism, along with profit and drugs and the other trends in modern sport, have corrupted something precious. Ron Pickering was outspoken: 'Sport has to be a sanctuary. It has to be something bigger than everyday life and to have something to look up to. That's why values are so important and why we keep the Olympic torch burning even when people want to extinguish it.'

But not everyone thinks you have to look to the past for these values. The champion hurdler David Hemery found it easy to reconcile his own quiet Christian faith with his commitment to top-level athletics. 'To do one's best, to get the most out of oneself athletically can be a spiritual experience,' he said. 'I don't think we should look back. But there needs to be a re-education as to what sport can be in terms of personal growth. Sport still holds a lot that is intrinsically good and worthwhile. People can discover themselves and a purpose to life.'

Eric Liddell discovered his ultimate purpose not in sport but beyond it. There was undoubtedly a sense in which he was most fully himself, body and soul, when he was running to win; but what he also had, crucially, was the ability to let go. That, perhaps, is his most valuable lesson for modern sport.

Many years after his Olympic triumph, he gave a talk to a group of fellow internees in the Chinese camp where they were being held by the Japanese. He described his thrill at watching a race in which a hurdler had refused to take advantage of the gap left by a fallen hurdle and swerved to jump the adjoining one instead. The athlete did not win the race, but he had acted in the only spirit that counted.

'Sport is wonderful,' Liddell told his audience. 'The most wonderful part of it is not the almost superhuman achievements but the spirit in which it is done. Take away that spirit and it is dead.'

4

'None Can Pass You
But the Examiner'

As Eric Liddell prepared for his journey home from the Paris Olympics, two university dons in Edinburgh were hatching a plot over a cup of Sunday afternoon tea. One was the professor of Greek, Dr Mair; the other was responsible for the graduation ceremony that was to take place on Thursday 17 July, five days ahead. One of the graduands would be Eric Liddell, the hero of the Olympics, and the students would be expecting something special to mark the occasion. What could be done?

They approached the keeper of the Royal Botanic Garden in Edinburgh. Did he have anything in the way of wild olive leaves, by any chance? The keeper thought he could manage something: oleaster, perhaps, a garden derivative of the wild olive.

So the plans were laid. There would be not just a graduation ceremony but a crowning ceremony as well. The university's principal and vice-chancellor, Sir Alfred Ewing, responded to the idea with enthusiasm and the professor duly sat down with pen and dictionary to compose an elegant encomium in Greek. On 17 July 1924, *The Scotsman* informed its readers that a special graduation ceremony was to take place at Edinburgh University that day: Eric Liddell was to be crowned with an olive wreath in honour of his Olympic victory.

The domed McEwan Hall in Edinburgh, donated to the university by the brewery family, had long been the venue for graduations and degree examinations. Over the years, successive generations of students had sat in serried ranks waiting to be capped, or letting their eyes wander over its magnificent decorations in a desperate search for exam inspiration. In the dome were fifteen figures representing the arts and sciences, painted against a background of gold to create the effect of an enamelled jewel, with an inscription designed to edify: 'Wisdom is the principal thing; therefore get wisdom; and with all thy getting, get understanding. Exalt her, and she shall bring thee honour.'

Over the top of the imposing platform, and on either side of it, they could gaze at huge fresco panels: Minerva, the tutelary deity of the university, seated upon a marble throne in the Grove of Academia, receiving the gift of the building itself; the Temple of Fame, showing nearly a hundred assorted philosophers and students attending a triple throne occupied by the three goddesses representing science, art and literature; and a panel depicting Fame crowning Success.

Rarely can the McEwan Hall decorations have seen a more appropriate occasion: Fame had indeed crowned Success, and Edinburgh University was not going to let anyone forget it. Several distinguished figures were present that morning to receive honorary degrees, including G.M. Trevelyan, the historian, Lord Macmillan, Sir Frederick Whyte, economist and sociologist Mrs Sidney Webb and Sir Owen Seaman, the editor of *Punch*. But none of them had any illusions: this was going to be Eric Liddell's day.

The Scotsman reported the following morning:

> It was quite apparent that those present had been reserving themselves to greet the Olympic victor. As Mr Liddell stepped forward to receive the ordinary degree of Bachelor of Science, the vast audience rose and cheered him to the echo. The cheering continued for an appreciable time and there were several calls for silence before Sir Alfred Ewing could make himself heard.

When the principal and vice-chancellor eventually managed to get a hearing, he produced a *bon mot* he must have been delighted with and which has now been immortalised in the Liddell legend. 'Mr Liddell,' he said, 'you have shown that none can pass you but the examiner.' Sir Alfred continued:

> In the ancient Olympic tests the victor was crowned with wild olive by the high priest of Zeus, and a poem written in his honour was presented to him. A vice-chancellor is no high priest, but he speaks and acts for the university; and in the name of the university, to which you have brought fresh honour, I present you with this epigram in Greek, composed by Professor Mair, and place upon your head this chaplet of wild olive.

The cheering was ecstatic. As the wreath was placed on Eric Liddell's lowered head, the Greek scroll containing the fruits of Professor Mair's labours was put in his hand. It was probably unintelligible to Eric himself, who had studied science, not the humanities, but translated, it read:

Graduation day, Edinburgh, July 1924.

Happy the man who the wreathed games essaying
Returns with laurelled brow,
Thrice happy victor thou, such speed displaying
As none hath showed till now;
We joy, and Alma Mater, for thy merit
Proffers to thee this crown:
Take it, Olympic Victor. While you wear it
May Heaven never frown.

Outside the McEwan Hall, the students grabbed Eric and carried him in a sedan-chair on their shoulders along the Edinburgh streets to St Giles Cathedral, where the traditional graduation service was to be held. In the newspaper photographs of Eric Liddell that day he was clearly enjoying himself, perched in his gown and hood on the victory chair, scroll in hand, wreath on head and with an enormous grin across his face.

The photographs say a great deal about Eric Liddell. Yes, he was modest. Yes, he slipped away from the Olympic arena to pray after his race, instead of joining the victory party. Yes, he wore his ordinary old suit to the dinner in his honour because it did not occur to him to wear anything else. But there was not a scrap of pious asceticism in him. In the photographs you do not see a man who is enjoying the attention but trying to pretend that he's not, or a man whose mind is on loftier things than a noisy student carnival, or who is embarrassed at being admired when earthly glory, as the preacher always saith, is vanity. Eric Liddell is simply enjoying himself. He knew how to savour life.

By the time they reached the steps of St Giles, the medieval church whose stones have witnessed so much of Scotland's history, another crowd had gathered, and a speech was called for. Liddell talked to them about the words inscribed over the gate of Pennsylvania University: 'In the dust of defeat as well as in the laurels of victory there is a glory to be found if one has done his best.' Those who had done their best and failed to win the laurels, said Eric, were owed as much honour as those who received them.

Sir Richard Lodge, the historian, said at the graduation lunch that he could not remember so much of the ancient Greek spirit about Edinburgh as he had noted that day, and proposed a toast to 'our Olympic victor'. Eric's reply made them laugh. He said that he was a short-distance runner owing to a defect in his constitution. He was extremely short-winded and therefore he would not keep them long. He blamed his unorthodox running style on his ancestors, who as Scottish Borderers were wont to make the odd foray into England and return rather faster than they went. That capacity for speed seemed to have been handed down from generation to generation, he said, and nobody looked for stylishness in a returning raider.

He ended by reminding them that a man was composed of three parts, body, mind and soul, and it was only when they educated each part in harmony that they would get the best and truest graduates from the university.

At the end of the lunch, a team of university 'Blues' drew up in a carriage. Eric and the principal were invited inside and off they went, escorted by hundreds of students from all the faculties. With Eric still wearing his olive wreath, the procession toured the city. They trooped along the historic Royal Mile and down to Princes Street, Edinburgh's main thoroughfare. As crowds milled around them, the police entered into the spirit of the proceedings and allowed the carriage on to the pavement.

They ended up outside the principal's house, where yet another crowd had materialised. Before they all went in for tea, Sir Alfred Ewing told the audience with a chuckle that he had never in his life basked in so much reflected glory in one day.

But the Olympic celebrations still had plenty of mileage in them. The next day Eric had to sit through another series of eulogies at a public dinner in his honour. He may have enjoyed the fun of being carted round by his fellow-students, but listening to glowing tributes was something he always found hard to bear. Dr Norman MacLean, of St Cuthbert's Parish Church in Edinburgh, described in *The Scotsman* Liddell's reply to the speeches made in his honour at that dinner:

> The shouting and the cheering suddenly ceased, and he began to speak. The modesty and simplicity and directness of his words went straight to the heart. No adulation, no fame, no flattery can ever affect this youth with the clean-cut features, the level eyes, and the soft voice. He has got that great redeeming gift, the gift of humour... He made us quickly realise that running was not to be his career. He was training to be a missionary in China, and he was to devote all his spare time until he set forth for the East in evangelistic work among the young men in Scotland.

Dr MacLean was getting into his stride. 'What a hush suddenly fell,' he wrote, his prose turning a deeper shade of purple. 'The Olympic Games were forgotten; the olive crowns and the thunder of the cheers; and we saw this young man go forth on his mission.'

You are spared the tributes that emanated from the Lord Provost's complimentary luncheon the following week, though no one spared Eric. However, he replied to the compliments and the presentation of an inscribed gold watch and chain from the Corporation of Edinburgh with customary grace and humour. Among the guests at the lunch that day were his friends D.P. Thomson and Tom McKerchar, to whom he paid fulsome tribute of his own. Looking towards McKerchar, he said:

> In all the mentions of my Olympic victory, one thing has been forgotten and that is the great part my trainer, Mr Tom McKerchar, has played in my success. For the last four years, he has coached me and shown me exactly how to run the various races. When I ran my first quarter mile at Edinburgh University, my trainer really ran it for me, before sending me out to try it on the track. I have much for which to thank Mr McKerchar in all my success.

His words were greeted by thunderous applause, as was a speech by Lord Sands which made a point of celebrating not so much his speed as a runner but the way he had put principle before career. 'There are greater issues in life than sport,' said his Lordship, 'and the greatest of these is loyalty to the great laws of the soul.'

Liddell's university peers were no less fervent in their admiration. A column in the Edinburgh University undergraduate magazine, *The Student*, shows just how infectious Liddell's charm must have been, and how impressed his fellow students were not just by what he had done but by the manner of the achievement:

Success in athletics sufficient to turn the head of any ordinary man, has left Liddell absolutely unspoilt, and his modesty is entirely genuine and unaffected. He has taken his triumphs in his stride, as it were, and has never made any sort of fuss. What he has thought it right to do, that he has done, looking neither to the left nor to the right, and yielding not one jot or tittle of principle either to court applause or to placate criticism. Courteous and affable, he is utterly free from 'gush'. Devoted to his principles, he is without a touch of Pharisaism. The best that can be said of any student is that he has left the fame of his university fairer than he found it, and his grateful Alma Mater is proud to recognise that to no man does that praise more certainly belong than to Eric Henry Liddell.

Between his university coronation and the Lord Provost's luncheon the next week, Liddell took the train to London. On 19 July, still just a few days after his Olympic triumph, he showed that his glorious running in Paris had been no fluke. In the British Empire *v.* USA contest at Stamford Bridge, he ran the final leg of the 4 x 440 yards relay race in a time that was reckoned to be under 48 seconds and possibly as low as 46 seconds. He started the leg about five yards behind his old American rival, Horatio Fitch, and beat him by a stride. It was an outstanding race.

A year later he carried off his last athletics appearance in Scotland with his usual flair. It was described afterwards by Professor Neil Campbell as a performance 'of uninterrupted triumph'. A crowd of 12,000 were at the Scottish Amateur Athletic Association meeting at Hampden Park in Glasgow in June to see him equal his own Scottish record time of 10.0 seconds in the 100 yards. They also watched him storm home in 22.2 seconds in the 220 yards, and in 49.2 seconds in the 440 yards (these were also both best Championship performances). It was the first time that 50 seconds had been broken at the Scottish Championships, and the feat was not to be repeated until 1937 or bettered until 1957.

Liddell was only the fourth athlete ever to have won the three short races together at the SAAA. The Jamaican Scot Alf Downer managed it three times in 1893, 1894 and 1895 before turning professional;

Eric Liddell winning the relay race for the British Empire against USA at Stamford Bridge, 19 July 1924.

W.H. Welsh and Wyndham Halswelle (the man who won Britain's first Olympic gold for the 400 metres in 1908) achieved the three Scottish titles in 1900 and 1906 respectively. Liddell achieved it twice at Hampden Park, in 1924 and again in 1925. And on this second occasion he was also a member of the winning relay team.

That competition, in the summer of 1925, was Liddell's last Scottish appearance. But there was plenty of leg-work in him yet, as the Chinese would soon be finding out.

5

'It Was Complete Hero-Worship'

After his Olympic triumph, Eric Liddell enrolled on a divinity course at the Scottish Congregational College in Edinburgh, where he spent his last year in Britain. The Congregational Church is doctrinally similar to the Church of Scotland, but the whole congregation participates in church government instead of delegating authority through the presbytery system. It was the church in which Eric had grown up. Now he was training to be a minister, with a view to going to China as a missionary at the end of the session.

Eric had long set his mind on returning to China. He had been born there, and there may have been something of the spirit of the place in his blood, perhaps even a trace of the ancient language silent on his tongue. Besides, his parents were there, his father still engaged on his life's work with the Chinese people, his sister Jenny and younger brother Ernest living there too. Already his elder brother Rob had gone back as a medical missionary. Eric wanted to spend his life sharing his faith, and so he turned, like them, to China.

Here again in Eric's life there was none of the heart-searching for which the storyteller is always hunting. There seems to have been no particular wrestling with the lure of stardom, no dark night of the soul, no dream with beckoning Chinese figures, no verse from Isaiah. There is not so much as a note from D.P. Thomson, who is usually so helpful, to record a climactic moment when Eric might have come up to him to announce, 'I'm going to China. I decided last night.'

Eric just always seems to have known that this was what he would do. He kept his studies up at university because he knew he needed a degree to be useful as a teacher in China. He enrolled at the Scottish Congregational College on his return from the Olympics so that he would have a theological qualification under his belt, too. The Anglo-Chinese College in Tientsin, to which he had been provisionally appointed, wanted him to share in the religious work as well as teach science and supervise athletics.

It was a hectic year. In addition to attending classes, much of his time was spent far from the college in theatres, music halls, churches, schools, auditoriums and other colleges all over Scotland and occasionally in England. This was the year in which he became fully associated with the student evangelistic campaigns.

These student campaigns were a phenomenon of the 1920s which left a deep mark on the religious life of Scotland. It is difficult nowadays to imagine the days when the minutiae of church affairs were splashed, or at least liberally sprinkled, over the newspapers every day. There were reports of Mission to Lepers meetings and missionary federations and every conceivable church society. The churches' loud demands for stricter drinking laws constantly dominated the headlines. Churchmen's views were courted by a respectful press.

It is equally difficult to visualise the impact of a handful of students who in 1922 started touring the country at weekends, trying to inject some life into the staid Scottish Kirk. In September 1924 the *Ardrossan and Saltcoats Herald* opined:

> Several students from Glasgow University are in Ardrossan this week conducting an evangelistic campaign, and consequently we are hearing fresh voices, if not a new Gospel. Whether staid and respectable church-going folk are disposed to agree with all the methods of the students or not, we think that such campaigns are needed in these days.

In another issue the same paper enthused:

> Their theme is familiar enough, but they have come with fresh enthusiasm to present it in their way and from their own angle. They preach a strong, virile message, related to the needs and problems of the day, which they believe to be essential to right the wrongs and transform the life of individuals and society.

The *Airdrie and Coatbridge Advertiser* was impressed by the numbers who flocked to the mass meetings and much uplifted by the spectacle of the local church being filled every evening of the week with 'an eager and expectant congregation'. Meanwhile, a columnist in one of the Wishaw papers was full of admiration for the rippling muscles of these young Apollos:

The students are a group of eager, alert, bustling, athletic and well-developed young men, full of enthusiasm and the strength of their own convictions, talking in a manner confident and inspiring, to people many years their seniors, yet with a wonderful power of appeal and magnetic attraction. Far from being kill-joys or milk-sops, these lads represent all that is manly and upright.

The leader of the band was our old friend D.P. Thomson. Back in 1921, Thomson had been present at a Seamen's Mission in Fraserburgh, a fishing town on Scotland's north-east coast, which was sending out signals of 'something happening' in the Church. Reports tell of one meeting where the church was so crammed that young men invaded the pulpit steps to hear the message.

It was their experience in this Fraserburgh Revival that led D.P. Thomson and friends to launch the Glasgow Students' Evangelistic Union (GSEU), perhaps the most vital force in evangelism in the 1920s. Walking down the main street of a Scottish town in these days, you would be likely to meet a notice like this somewhere along the way:

CAMPAIGN FORTNIGHT IN KILMARNOCK
September 20-October 5
Keep these dates free.
WHY? WHAT'S ON?
The students are coming!!!
WHERE FROM?
Glasgow, Edinburgh and St Andrews –
the Universities and the Colleges
WHAT FOR? WAIT AND SEE!

If there was a special meeting in the campaign, you might find the words in bold capitals: 'SPEAKER: MR ERIC H. LIDDELL, OLYMPIC ATHLETE'. Eric had been taking part in these campaigns ever since the meeting at Armadale in April 1923. He and D.P. would address Glasgow schoolboys and Tyneside men's associations, church women's groups and, on one occasion, the imbibing customers of a Sunday hostelry.

Eric was studying during the day and dashing off every evening and all weekend either to the running track or to speak in some obscure church hall. He could never say no. His style of oratory remained as flat as ever, and its effect just as mysteriously potent. He continued to tell his young audiences simple stories, parables almost, illustrations garnered from the chemistry lab, the rugby pitch and the running-track. They continued to follow him.

'I think it was just a very simple Christian message,' said Mrs Elsa Watson, who as young Elsa McKechnie was busy planning to set up his fan club around this time:

> There was no difficult theology to understand. All that he said, as far as I can remember, I could write on the back of a post-card. But I understood what he was talking about, and invariably in churches I have not understood what ministers are talking about. He talked about what you were going to do tomorrow, and what you were thinking today, and his honesty was just flashing out there the whole time.

Eric became the president of the Edinburgh branch of the GSEU in the spring of 1925. By this time, the 'Manhood Campaigns', as they were called, were in full swing. It sounds faintly suspect today, but the idea of these was to show young men that you didn't need to be a mummy's boy to be a Christian. Eric Liddell – handsome, manly and athletic – was a godsend to the movement. 'Muscular Christianity' was the phrase on everyone's lips.

'Playing the game of life in a manly and Christian way,' was how the *Glasgow Herald* described one student team's message in a campaign in Barrhead, Renfrewshire:

> Their leader, Eric Liddell, has struck that note in all his addresses. He stands for the Christian youth with a clean breeze about him, and his lungs well filled with the air that blows from the Judaean hills. There is not a tincture of conventional piety about any of them; they are interesting and winning. We wish them all the best kinds of success and a closing service that will crown their eight-day effort.

What Eric and his Judaean lungs thought about that encomium is not recorded. Nor his reaction to a poem in another of the local newspapers, believed to have been penned by an adoring daughter of the manse:

ERIC LIDDELL!
To Barrhead comes a gallant man,
Who in Olympic races ran,
Gained first prize, and led the van –
Victorious Eric Liddell!

Graduation day, Edinburgh, July 1924.

He comes a nobler race to run,
To strive for Master's prize – 'Well done,'
Which he'll deserve when duly won –
Undaunted Eric Liddell!

True soldier of the Cross thou art,
To fight 'gainst wrong, and take the part
Of sinners struck by Satan's dart –
Great-hearted Eric Liddell!

Eric Liddell had plenty of practice in deflecting the arrows of hero-worship which came zinging towards him wherever he went. And it wasn't just daughters of the manse firing them off. Elsa McKechnie, who must take the prize for sheer dedication to the job, was rather less interested in Liddell's muscular Christianity than his muscular arms, not to mention his twinkling eyes and kind smile. She called the effect he had on impressionable girls 'the Beatle-mania of the day'.

Elsa was fourteen when she first came across Eric Liddell at Morningside Congregational Church in Edinburgh. 'I remember hearing him and seeing him and thinking that this was someone worth doing something about. I went to some of his meetings and then I decided to form an Eric Liddell Club.' Nearly sixty years later, Elsa McKechnie, by then Mrs Watson, could produce with a flourish the rules of the club whose membership comprised all her best friends at George Watson's Ladies' College. The piece of paper from a school exercise-book announced, in the neatest of schoolgirl scripts, the following:

(1) Each member is entitled to one page of this book, in which a poem, or account of ERIC LIDDELL must be inserted, which must be approved of by the committee.

(2) Before becoming a member of this club, the person in question must undergo an oral examination, put by the founder.

(3) Each member must promise three things. i) Always to uphold ERIC LIDDELL ii) To attend all meetings arranged by the committee. iii) To keep all rules of the club. It is also desirable that members should use the ERIC LIDDELL line.

(4) Members will be presented with a photo of ERIC LIDDELL and must promise to put it in a place of honour.

(5) Should any member of this club do anything unworthy of the club, the committee will at once expel the member in question.
BY ORDER

The object of all this fervour wrote back from his new post in Tientsin on 17 December 1925 to acknowledge the founding of the club. 'I do not know what I might be let in for!!!' wrote Eric in his polite, rather awkward style, peppered as always with triple exclamation marks. 'However, there are times when we have to risk a little and after due consideration I have decided to accept the honour you have given me. You will find my name signed and the date on a piece of paper enclosed.'

Before he left for China, Elsa had dogged him faithfully around Edinburgh and one day plucked up the courage to invite him to tea:

> I asked off early from school and cycled home at top speed. I think my family were all hugely amused. But he came, which was so typical of him, to be kind and considerate to a youngster. I don't think I ate or drank a thing. After he went away I got his teacup and I emptied all the tea leaves into an envelope and put it into an album I kept. I also remember keeping the paper and string of a parcel he sent me. I think Eric looked on it all in a very kindly way, as he did with everything. I think he probably understood.

He did. He answered all her letters, patiently and formally, in his neat, carefully formed handwriting:

> YMCA c/o Sutties,
> 26 Bedford Place,
> London,
> 22.iv.25
> Dear Elsa,
> It was so good of you to send me that Easter card also the two p.c.' s. I'm awfully glad you are enjoying your time at Biggar. It must be delightful to get out into the fresh air especially on a farm.
> As you see by my address I am in that 'little village' known as London. I am to be here until the beginning of May when I return to Edinburgh. My holiday has been most enjoyable. Our term closed at the beginning of April. After that I went to Barrhead with eight or nine students and had a campaign there. We slept in one of the church Halls and looked after some of our meals ourselves, although we always went out for dinner.
> It was strenuous but worth while, and I enjoyed every minute. After that I went to Aberdeen for four days Dundee for one and now I am here.
> With the very best wishes for a glorious holiday. So glad your 'cup is running over'.
> Yours very sincerely
> Eric H. Liddell

'Was it adoration?' Elsa Watson mused:

> I don't really know what it was. I know one thing: it wasn't trying to grab him for oneself. I suppose it was adoration. Yet it was a pretty dignified

thing for fourteen-year-olds. There was no shouting or screaming. It was complete hero-worship. We used to wait, some of us, outside Hope Terrace just to see him coming along.

Looking back I don't suppose Eric was a wonderful public speaker. But he was so sincere and so electric. I mean, he shone. It wasn't like just going to listen to a good speaker.

Years later, Elsa was still writing to Eric. She had become a friend of the family, and when his fiancée visited Scotland without him one summer he wrote to Elsa asking her to look after Florence, who was two years younger than Elsa. When Elsa married in 1939, Eric sent her a lithographed picture by a Chinese artist he had saved from death. It was a peony, the flower of China, and he sent it because he liked the beauty of the image and the words on it: 'She is the most beautiful in the city (China); her modesty and manner come from God.'

Elsa Watson was quick to leap to her hero's defence when the point was put to her that Liddell was not averse to holding forth on Temperance Society platforms: did that not make him a bit of a kill-joy, a moral tub-thumper? 'Oh, Eric was never that,' she said. 'I don't think he ever went in for tirades against anyone. I think this was one of the reasons he was so effective. He put it in such a humble way, more a matter of suggestion than anything else.'

That was certainly not the opinion of an irate gentleman who wrote to the editor of a Scottish newspaper complaining of Mr Liddell's intolerant language. It is the only note of acrimony about Eric Liddell that research has unearthed:

MODERATE DRINKING
A REPLY TO MR ERIC LIDDELL
TO THE EDITOR:
I am one of those who greatly admire Mr Eric Liddell as an athlete and sportsman; but it is with great regret that I observe that he has allied himself with narrow-minded, fanatical teetotallers... One can have no admiration for the person who advocates compulsory teetotalism for everybody. Having joined the extreme sect of total abstainers, Mr Liddell adopts their intolerant language. Witness his speech at a 'temperance rally' at Glasgow last week. He said – 'Drink took away from character; drink took away from a man all that was honourable.'

These statements are not in accord with fact. Applied to 'drink' per se they are untrue; applied to drinking in excess they are true.

There are thousands upon thousands of old athletes in the country
– runners, football players, cricketers, golfers and others – who have not
been abstainers, but who are living today in good health and prosperity,
useful upright citizens, admired and venerated by their fellow countrymen
for their honourable characters.

MODERATE DRINKER of 74 years.

The offending speech had been delivered at the annual temperance
rally of the Glasgow Presbytery in the City Hall. The attendance was
so great that an overflow meeting had had to be arranged. Liddell was
sharing the platform with another leading Scots athlete, Duncan Wright,
and a clutch of ministers. He told the audience that two of the greatest
problems the Church had to face were gambling and intemperance.
Both these evils were sapping the energy of their young people, and the
Church had to put up a united front or they would lose ground.

He believed drink had a lot to do with the length of life of the athlete,
and the abstainer could add a couple of years to his career. Temptation
came to both the athlete and the businessman when they were least able
to resist it. Drink took away from the character. Drink took away from
a man all that was honourable. In the context of the times, the message
was actually rather mild. Even today Liddell's views are not all that far
from those of the official bodies who are trying to do something about
the social cancer of alcoholism. Although Liddell's language is primarily
moral, his implications are social.

Public concern about the problems of pauperism, unemployment,
health and hygiene had continued to grow from its Victorian roots, till in
the 1920s it had become a powerful movement. Concern about drunkenness had not abated since Hogarth drew his admonitory 'Gin Lane' series.
Reformers of every school, social or spiritual, agreed that drunkenness
was one of the biggest social problems they had to contend with. If the
quality of life was to be improved, they argued, then drunkenness must be
suppressed, licences controlled, and the masses educated and restrained.

While temperance and abstinence societies proliferated in this country,
the United States was imposing total prohibition of drink on its citizens.
The problems of drink were debated *ad infinitum* in the British press,
with an impressive barrage of statistical reports on the health risks of
alcohol. Anyone who doubts the seriousness of their convictions should
look at the famous speech of Lloyd George in 1915, when a deputation
from the Shipbuilders' Federation approached him on the subject. They
were worried about the effect of drunkenness on the war effort.

'In dealing with this evil,' Lloyd George replied, 'the feeling is that if we are to settle German militarism, we must first of all settle with the Drink. We are fighting Germany, Austria and Drink, and as far as I can see, the greatest of these deadly foes is Drink.'

Strong stuff. But not as strong as the Revd James Muir's pamphlet issued by the Church of Scotland in 1930, under the title *The Progress of Temperance in Scotland*. 'Civilization is only possible through temperance,' Mr Muir informed his readers:

> Temperance is faith's strong defence. Intemperance brings downfall and ruin, and the extinction of its light of love. Alcohol is the foe of the entire man, body, soul and spirit. His bodily functions are all worsened by it. His mind is inflamed, unbalanced and degraded. Conscience is stifled, affections hardened. A fleshly lust that wars against the soul is kindled by it.

This was doubtless the kind of 'narrow-minded, fanatical teetotaller' to which our 'Moderate Drinker of 74 years' objected. Eric Liddell had probably been influenced by that strain of thought, since it was especially prevalent among the missionary community in which he grew up: a belief, it seems, that to touch a drop of alcohol was a sign of moral weakness akin to indulging in an illicit sex binge. The principle was hammered home by some churchmen with a moral condescension which must have infuriated the folk who prided themselves on a temperate intake.

Liddell was too little of a dogmatist for any of that. He believed drink was bad for you, and he believed it enough to stand on a platform and tell people so. His speeches are studded with hackneyed epigrams like 'To abstain is safe; to drink leads to crime and poverty.' But, in general, he is coaxing his audience along with the suggestion that abstention has worked pretty well for him and it might reduce some of the appalling waste in Scottish society if more people tried it.

In the early summer of 1925, he made ready to leave for China. Enormous crowds turned up for the valedictory meetings in Edinburgh and Glasgow. The Glasgow occasion required an overflow meeting in a nearby church for nearly 1,000 people who had to be turned away. A few weeks previously, the last campaign meeting of the series had packed out the whole of Edinburgh's large Usher Hall, and then a neighbouring church; hundreds more had been turned away. On the Sunday before he left, two church services were held in his honour, and on the Monday he was astonished to find himself receiving the most amazing send-off any departing missionary can ever have received from Edinburgh's Waverley Station, or from anywhere else.

'That son of yours,' a family friend wrote to Eric's parents in China on 1 July, 'is so modest I fear he may not think to send you any echo of the many flattering things that happened to him last Sunday and Monday in Auld Reekie.' So the friend, a Mr Bryson, obliges instead. He tells them of the services at Morningside and in Augustine church:

> One of the most striking speeches was that of Professor Russell Scott. It was simply amazing to hear that teacher – not a man to wear his heart on his sleeve – openly acknowledge how he had been sitting at your son's feet, and of his dominant influence in the college. Dr Black said he simply loved your son, and declared he had preached a better sermon than all the ministers in Edinburgh.

The next day, the citizens of Edinburgh were treated to as colourful a spectacle as the one they had hurried along to see a year earlier. A carriage festooned with streamers and ribbons, drawn by a team of students, collected the departing hero at the door of the Scottish Congregational College in Hope Terrace and headed for Waverley Station. Traffic in the city centre stopped as the crowds began to spill on to the street. Some of them were singing. The soaring melody of the Scots song composed in honour of another romantic Scots hero, the Jacobite Bonnie Prince Charlie, reached Liddell's ears as the carriage jogged past. 'Better loved ye canna be,' they sang. 'Will ye no' come back again.'

Inside the station, Eric was swept along the platform to his train. People were laughing and crying and shouting. When they clamoured for a speech, he stood up and thanked everyone for the send-off. He said he was going abroad to try and play his part in the great task of unifying the countries of the world under Christ, and he hoped everyone at home would do their bit too. Soon someone started up the singing again. Mr Bryson thought it was Eric himself who began the hymn 'Jesus Shall Reign Where'er the Sun'. Whoever did, it soon had the entire station belting out hymn after hymn as the train gathered steam and finally pulled out.

'It was such a send-off as no missionary going abroad has ever had in Edinburgh,' Mr Bryson wrote. 'I was glad to be there.'

6

'A Fellow's Life Counts for Far More at This'

When Eric Liddell arrived in Tientsin, his pupils were on strike. Far behind him lay beautiful, genteel Edinburgh with its hills and its castle, its New and Old Towns, its university and churches, summer sales and well-appointed tea-rooms. Behind him were the adoring autograph-hunters and a stream of tempting offers of lucrative teaching posts in top-drawer schools. In front of him lay the large, sprawling and unlovely Tientsin, capital of the province of Hopei, a divided and confused city in the north-east of a divided, confused and angry country.

In 1925, Tientsin was already a busy inland port some sixty miles south-east of Peking (now Beijing), lying on the banks of the River Haihe, a river which overflowed its banks nearly every year with often catastrophic results. Tientsin had been developing rapidly during the twentieth century and could boast a growing population of about a million people; today Tianjin, as it is known now, is the third largest city in mainland China, second only to Shanghai for industry and commerce, with a population that by the end of 2004 had risen to 10.24 million.

Three main railway lines converged on the city in which Eric was to spend the next twelve years, and it was the terminal for the Trans-Siberian Railway. Seven newspapers hit the streets daily. Electric trams ran over macadamised roads. Miles of wharves teemed with coolies unloading ships from all over the Far East, and crowded suburbs stretched in every direction. It was a city of sharp contrasts. The climate, though not unhealthy with its sea-breezes blowing in from the coast thirty miles away, was one of extremes, with dry, snowless winters caused by the Siberian anticyclone and hot humid summers often marked by heavy rainfalls in July and August. When these summer mini-monsoons failed, there were droughts; when they were over-generous, there were equally devastating floods. Occasional violent north winds from Mongolia could bring dust-storms in the spring.

Just as stark were the contrasts in the lives and lifestyles of the inhabitants. Mansions rubbed shoulders with hovels; three universities and scores of schools co-existed with widespread illiteracy and age-old superstition. Ex-presidents, retired generals, politicians in retreat, commercial tycoons, leaders of the intelligentsia and sophisticated socialites lived almost next door to sailors and shopkeepers, factory workers and peasants. Almost next door, but not exactly, for Tientsin, 'City of the Celestial Ford', was really two cities, not one.

The first was the old Chinese city with its network of tiny lanes, the equivalent of Edinburgh's Old Town, just to the north-west of the present city centre. It had formerly been surrounded by ancient walls dating back to the early fifteenth century and rebuilt in the nineteenth century, but these had been demolished in the aftermath of the Boxer Rising in 1901. The streets outside the old walls were named after the marketplaces that used to flourish there: Needle Market Street, Grain Market Street, Donkey Market Street, and so on. In the Devils' Market, antiques and stolen goods were on sale. There was an amusement quarter with theatres, jugglers and acrobats, and the whole place bustled with coolies, beggars, street-traders, visitors in rickshaws, workers from the salt-pans south of the town and sailors. There were sailors everywhere.

The large number of sailors frequenting Tientsin gave popularity to the worship of Tian hou (Celestial Queen), popularly known as the Good Mother. According to legend, she had been a sailor's daughter who saved her father from shipwreck by remote influence. A magnificent temple was built in her honour on the quayside just outside the east gate of the Old Town. Sailors flocked there to ask for her protection. In spring, pilgrimages were made to the temple, and each crew would bring a model of their ship. There were other temples in and around the Old Town, too, such as the Temple of Confucius, and more than a dozen mosques, headed by the Great Mosque to the north-west.

The other Tientsin was the European and Japanese town which grew rapidly round the concessionary areas that had been granted through treaties in the second half of the nineteenth century. These were all south-east of the old 'Chinese town', and lay on either side of the Haihe River. These concessions were, in effect, colonies, run by foreign consuls with their own troops and police forces; Chinese law did not operate inside them. Along the right bank of the river were the British and French concessions, granted in 1858, as well as the Japanese concession (granted after the Sino War in 1895) and the German concession of 1896 which came to an end in 1914. On the left bank was the huge

Russian concession, along with the Belgian and Italian concessions, and the Austro-Hungarian concession which also ended in 1914. The architecture was a cosmopolitan blend of all the European styles, so that a newcomer to this part of Tientsin would find himself travelling the length and breadth of Europe along Victoria Park and the Via Vittorio Emanuele, the Rue du Baron Gros and the Baron Czekam Strasse.

Colourful and cosmopolitan though they may have been, these concessions had mainly been wrested from the Chinese by force of arms. The foreigners so firmly entrenched in Tientsin were tolerated grudgingly. Ever since the sixteenth century, China had been a mecca for European traders and a magnet for European evangelists. This was the land of silk and tea, jade and gold, tempting trade-routes and abundant seaports, incense and ancient painted gods. And ever since the Portuguese and Spanish had first arrived in 1514, hungry for wealth and converts, the Chinese had looked upon all Westerners as marauding pirates, 'foreign devils'.

They had a point. No country was more diligent in seizing the chance of commercial piracy than trade-hungry Britain. Most notorious of all Britain's dealings with China was the opium trade. From the late eighteenth century, British merchants shipped India-grown opium into China in order to pay for Chinese tea and silk, which the Manchu Empire refused to exchange for anything but silver. When the Imperial Government eventually tried to suppress opium smoking, the British merchants refused to cooperate. In retaliation, some of them were shut into their factory in Canton in 1839 and had their stocks of opium destroyed. British warships responded, and the Opium War was on. It ended with the Chinese suing for peace in 1842. The Treaty of Nanking legalised the opium trade, opened up Canton and other ports, made the island of Hong Kong a British base, freed British subjects from Chinese law and gave them concession areas to live in. It was the first of what the Chinese called the 'Unequal Treaties'.

Despite the unpopularity of the British, their Protestant missionaries – with the Dutch and the Americans – did make ground among the sorely oppressed Chinese peasants. There was even a Christian-inspired rebellion, the Taiping Revolution, though this failed to win missionary support and was put down with the help of European military advisers. But if the Taiping Revolution failed, other popular movements were growing. More and more, the Chinese were beginning to protest against exploitation both by their own rulers and by the foreigners flooding the country with factory-made goods which upset the Chinese rural economy, putting thousands out of work and adding to the misery of life under a corrupt and inefficient administration. The Boxer Rising in 1900 was directed against the growing power of Western nations in China and involved attacks on foreigners, foreign imports and Chinese converts to Christianity. This was the frightening upheaval in which Eric Liddell's parents were caught up during the first year of their married life.

The Boxers invaded the legation quarter in Peking and the concessions in Tientsin. Eight countries, including Britain, sent a relief force of 30,000 troops. Their siege and bombardment of Tientsin and Peking broke the back of the Boxer Rising. There was much pillaging and plunder and slaughter. When it was all over in 1901, China had to pay an indemnity of 450 million taels of silver. More foreign concessions were granted, foreign garrisons were allowed to protect the legations and the Chinese people were burdened with heavier taxes to pay the indemnity. It was then that the walls of old Tientsin were demolished at the insistence of the Europeans, because the rebels had been entrenched behind them.

In 1911, a revolution led by the Western-educated Dr Sun Yat-sen ended the Manchu Empire and created a Chinese republic, presided over at first by a power-hungry warlord called Yuan Shi-kai. But this did nothing either to solve the power struggle in China or to alleviate the conditions of the people. Popular movements increased and there were more and more armed uprisings. After 1915, the number of strikes also increased rapidly. Between 1919 and 1921 there were more than 170 strikes involving 250,000 workers.

The real power was by then in the hands of hundreds of warlords who assumed control of whole areas of the country, levying taxes, raising private armies, fighting each other and then negotiating treaties. One warlord managed to put the last Manchu emperor, who had abdicated in 1912, back on the throne, although only for a week. Another warlord became dictator of Manchuria with Japanese help. The interminable military campaigns of the war-lords wrecked harvests and caused untold suffering among the people.

As if all that was not disruptive enough, China also chose to join the 1914-1918 war against Germany (although her one belligerent act was to send coolies to France, where they dug Allied trenches along the Western Front). The real trouble began after the war, when all Chinese hopes of winning some respect for their sovereignty and their territorial integrity were dashed by the Treaty of Versailles of 1919. The Allies allowed Japan to keep all her gains, and they themselves retained all their own pre-war concessions along the Chinese coast. The Chinese got nothing.

Anger and disgust at this betrayal by the Allies fuelled a nationalist demonstration known as the Fourth of May Movement, which in turn sparked off nationwide strike action. The Chinese Communist Party was born out of these protests in 1920. Among the delegates to the First National Congress of the Communist Party held in Shanghai that year was a young teacher called Mao Tse-tung. In 1922, Chinese strikers tied up all the British ships in Hong Kong, closed factories and paralysed the economy. Strikers near Kowloon were fired on by British troops with many casualties. In June 1925, not long before Eric Liddell arrived back in China, 100,000 Chinese went on strike in Hong Kong, and demonstrators were fired on by British and French warships in an incident known as the 'Shakee Massacre'.

By July 1925, the Canton Revolutionary Government was calling itself the National Government, and its army had started to challenge the warlords in the east. But the revolutionary surge in China was divided into two distinct factions. One was the Kuomintang, the Nationalist Party founded by Sun Yat-sen and now led by Chiang Kai-shek; they favoured a strong national state. The other was the Communists, who wanted a complete transformation of society. These two factions would soon be at each other's throats in another civil war. They would also, before long, be facing invasion from the Japanese, who were already encroaching on Chinese territory in the north-east.

This was the confused, suffering land in which Eric Liddell found himself in the summer of 1925. His father had warned him what to expect. In his 1924 missionary report from China, the Revd James Liddell had written:

> To those who look on it seems that no one party is strong enough to command obedience, and really govern the country. The government of any one party is flouted by some other, although that other may have sworn loyalty to the one in power. It's not surprising that during part of this year Church work has been so difficult.
>
> This year we have had the triple evils of war, flood and famine. Any one of these is bad enough, but all three together have made for suffering that is very hard to realise. Ruin has overtaken great numbers of families, and it will never be known how many lives have been lost, through these visitations. Oh, the horror of it all! And to think that so much of it is needless suffering and waste.

Mr Liddell's latest report had made even gloomier reading:

> Words fail to convey to one not conversant with ways Chinese the
> conditions that exist to make a forecast impossible. The grievances of
> China have been magnified beyond all recognition. So complex is the
> situation, so varied are the views expressed, so opposite the conclusions
> reached, so many the solutions suggested, that one staggers beneath the
> crushing load. A nation is in travail, seeking to reproduce that which
> will meet all its aspirations. Whether it will do so or not is another
> question.

Eric had both reports with him on the long train journey east. The China
that he had left Edinburgh for was a powder-keg about to explode.

On its way to Tientsin, the Trans-Siberian Railway passed through the
summer resort of Pei-tai-ho, still the popular playground for Westerners
that it had been in Eric's childhood. Eric left the train there to join
his family, who were taking a holiday in one of the mission-owned
bungalows away from the stifling city heat. Among the welcoming party
at the station were some of his future colleagues from the Tientsin
Anglo-Chinese College. In some embarrassment they explained to the
eager new teacher that the college was currently being boycotted. Some
of the students had been intimidated, they told him. The 'May 30th'
movement in Shanghai had sent out waves of unrest, which Tientsin
was still feeling.

The trouble had started on 14 May, when workers in a Japanese-owned
cotton mill in Shanghai went on strike in protest at the dismissal of
Chinese workers. The protest was taken up by the students, who demon-
strated on 30 May and were fired on by the British police. After this 'May
30th massacre', the Communist Party called on all Shanghai workers,
merchants and students to strike. 'Oppose imperialism' was the slogan.
The strikes and boycotts fanned out from Shanghai to other centres of
foreign concentration like Tientsin, where the Anglo-Chinese College,
run by the London Missionary Society, was an obvious target.

The college was the leading British school in North China, a beautiful, grey, towered building on Tientsin's Taku Road. Its 500 pupils were
from the middle to upper social class of Chinese families. The school had
been founded to cater for the wealthier and more influential element in
the population, a group for which missionary societies had made little
provision as a rule. The idea was both to offer a top academic training
and to teach Christian values to the future leaders of Chinese society.

Teaching was in English and organised on an intimate tutorial system, with a staff of five British and twenty-five Chinese masters. Every year the college turned out forty or fifty graduates, who either continued to universities in China or the West, or went straight into the civil service, business or politics.

As well as emphasising academic achievement and Christian studies, the college was a pioneer of sports in North China. When Dr Lavington Hart founded the college in 1902, it was unheard of for a student to discard his long, blue cotton gown and go chasing after a ball or an athletic record; it offended every idea of decorum in the Chinese tradition. It was the mission schools who pioneered the concept of serious sport and the British ideal of sportsmanship and fair play. Liddell said later:

> About fifty of the five hundred Chinese Pupils are boarders, while, of the staff, four are British and fifteen or twenty are Chinese. On the sporting side the boys play 'soccer', but western games have not yet taken on very much. They are, however, beginning to increase in popularity, and goal posts can be seen on many open spaces.
>
> I do not think that Rugby will ever become a game for the Chinese, for the conditions are too severe… the temperature often dropping to 30 degrees of frost. In spite of this, there are British and French Army teams, and a local team of foreigners. Here and there you come across some good 'soccer' players, and there have been Chinese members of Tientsin teams playing against Shanghai and at other places. Although this is the exception rather than the rule, it is an indication that the Chinese are capable of playing our games.
>
> At the present moment, however, the unsettled state of the country makes it very difficult to stage any programme of sports.

Once they did overcome their distaste, the Chinese idea of sporting endeavour was to play football tripping over their gowns, rush inside at the first drop of rain, refuse to begin the game if they reckoned their side's chances were anything less than a hundred to one, leave the field in high dudgeon with the entire team if a shin was kicked, and dispute vociferously with the referee. This sounds a lot of fun, but was not to be tolerated by the zealous British. The mission schools saw their championship of sporting play as the highest moral calling. 'It is one of the most productive fields for Christian work,' wrote one of Eric's colleagues, A.P. Cullen, in *Making China's Men*:

Family group, *c.* 1925.

for it remains generally true that the man who is a real sportsman in athletics, who can play the game under all circumstances, fight against odds and disappointments without losing heart or temper, and knows how to take a beating – he is the man who is most likely to be a true sportsman in the greater game of life.

This was just the job for Eric. But, unfortunately, the students were not even playing the game of lessons right now. The staff had a meeting at Pei-tai-ho and decided to put a bold face on the boycott and try to open the college as usual in September, after the summer break. They all returned to Tientsin to prepare for the new term and Eric joined his mother, father, sister Jenny and thirteen-year-old brother Ernest at No. 6 London Mission, their spacious house in the French concession, where the London Missionary Society had based its operations.

The London Missionary Society had been in China since 1807. The LMS Congregationalists were among the first Protestant missions to sail east after the sudden upsurge of British evangelical activity at the end of the eighteenth century. During the next century they were joined by the Baptists, the English Presbyterians, the Anglicans, the Methodists, the Scots Presbyterians, the Quakers, the Plymouth Brethren and, in 1860, the non-denominational China Inland Mission. Jesuits, Dominicans, Franciscans and Augustinians had already been along with the Catholic version.

Before the end of the nineteenth century, the Protestant missions had penetrated every province of China, although they had reached only a small proportion of the Chinese population. In the 1920s their activity still remained largely concentrated on the east coast provinces, where four fifths of the 8,000 or so missionaries were working. Most missionary societies refrained from evangelising on each other's patch, but many Chinese found the profusion of denominations perplexing. Catholic and Protestant missions, rarely close, were sometimes in bitter competition for congregations.

From early times, the presence of missionaries had aroused antagonism in China, partly because of the conflict with traditional habits of thought, but more from the growing national sentiment against anything Western. As Evan Luard says in *Britain and China*:

> The missionary was one of the tribulations imposed by western imperialism. Like railways, extra-territorial rights and foreign control of the Customs, he became a symbol of Chinese humiliation; and those who adopted his faith began to be seen as traitors to the Chinese cause.

In the late nineteenth century, missions were attacked, missionaries massacred and scurrilous propaganda against them circulated. It culminated in the slaughter inspired by the Boxer Rising. Eric Liddell had been born as the anger of that time was just dying; he returned to China as the next wave of hostility against the missionaries was beginning to break. An 'Anti-Christian Movement' was initiated by the increasingly nationalistic Chinese. Missionaries were condemned as imperialists in disguise and Chinese Christians as their lackeys. In country areas, some were attacked; in the towns, missionary hospitals and schools were subjected to strikes and boycotts.

All this was tough on the missionaries, who had come to China neither to further the aims of their governments nor to support popular rebellions, but to preach a non-political salvation. The societies had rigid rules about not getting involved in politics, and no missionary felt he had the right to speak out against the policies of his own government or any other, though it may be fair to wonder if some unconsciously used the 'no-politics' rule to escape difficult decisions about the practical implications of the non-materialistic, peace-serving message they were preaching. The missionaries were living, after all, in comfortable houses in the cosy, socially self-contained community of a foreign concession, wrested and maintained by force of arms, while their potential converts were literally slumming it down the road.

But what could they do? It was a colonial lifestyle that the missionaries did not invent and could do little to change, although Eric Liddell reported later that they supported moves for a gradual handing back of the concessions. The missionaries did also take a stand against the opium smoking with which their greedy governments had cursed the Chinese. It was unfortunate that they had to live in the kind of house Eric now shared with his family at No. 6 London Mission: big and roomy with a tennis court in front, in a concession guarded by troops and police against any Chinese annoyances. It made the missionaries all too easy to associate with everything that was most hated in China.

Seen as a clique, as an exclusive social group in their western compound, the missionaries must have seemed an unattractive group at times. Individually, though, they were often loved by the Chinese who knew them. They worked tirelessly, caring for and loving the people they worked with. When the attacks came, the missionaries were often protected by the people they served.

Eric started his first job as a missionary teacher in September. The staff of the Anglo-Chinese College were gratified to see 150 of the 400 students registering that morning, and as many again over the next few weeks. The school was back in business. Eric was there to teach pure science with chemistry as his special subject, and in his methodical way he began immediately to prepare his lectures and stock up the college laboratory. He was asked to take a few English classes as well, which made him smile. English had never really been his subject.

He was expected, too, to contribute to the religious life of the college, which he did with gusto. Every morning there was a service of worship, at which one of the British teachers spoke on the day's scripture passage. Eric's gift of commanding attention with the simplest of talks quickly made him the most popular of the speakers with the boys. Each tutor also held a weekly Bible circle for his class outside school hours. Eric, never one to stand on formality, brought the pupils to his own house.

He did not make remarkable progress as a teacher. He was never at his best standing in front of a class trying to impart organised information. 'I never seemed to get a real grip of the class,' he admitted once with some dejection. The schoolmaster's role was too starchy for Eric. He adored children and loved being with them, but not in the formal, authoritarian role of the teacher. He preferred to be laughing with them, helping them to run faster, telling them stories, inspiring, teasing and encouraging. He worked hard at the role, though, determined as ever to make a go of whatever he put his mind to. His headmaster reported much later that 'as the years have rolled by the momentum has steadily increased'. He had begun to develop the technique.

On the sports field it was a different matter. Eric took over the college athletics and soon had his boys breaking records. He also found time to do some running himself and was soon competing regularly in his long navy blue shorts (in an era of flapping shorts, Eric's always seemed to look longer than anyone else's) against the foreign troops who guarded the concessions. The first time he ran in Tientsin, spectators who had never seen Liddell in action gaped. It was a relay race, and he streaked away so fast that he picked up thirty yards in the last lap and beat the crack runner of the 15th US Cavalry.

He also lost no time in joining the troops' rugby matches. Rugby in Tientsin was about the most uncomfortable game you could play. The wind came biting down from the Gobi Desert in the north, whipping up the soft, flaky topsoil on their pitch, whisking it into the players' eyes and the cuts on their knees. Both sides were soon filthy with dust and grime. But the former Scottish internationalist revelled in the game and was soon reviving the elusive speed that had been so devastating on the Gracie–Liddell wing. One British soldier was once rash enough to try a lunge as he passed. 'Cor, like a blooming Seagrave,' he was heard to mutter as Eric zoomed away.

The athletics track was just as bad as the rugby pitch, and Eric was soon directing the reclamation of a large piece of land for a sports ground. Designs were based on the Stamford Bridge ground in London which had seen some of his most celebrated triumphs, and by the time the work was finished, Tientsin could boast one of the finest running tracks in the whole of the Far East. Eric himself was one of the first to compete there at the Annual International Athletic Games.

People in Britain had little idea of Liddell's athletic achievements in China. A booklet by the McWhirter brothers called *Get to Your Marks* gives a world ranking for the 400 metres in 1929: 'Liddell, E. – 49.0 secs:

date not known – somewhere in China.' He was certainly running well enough in China for the *Peking and Tientsin Times* to express surprise in October 1928 that he had not been invited to join the British Olympic team in Amsterdam that summer. According to the correspondent:

> The irony is that Liddell would have lent support in one of the weak links, the 400 metres representatives, and his value for the relay races can hardly be over-estimated. Only a few weeks back, the Scot turned in 21.8 for the 200 metres and 47.8 for the 400. Both these times represent the winning mark at Amsterdam, though neither is quite as good as Liddell's best. His 400 mark, of course, is a world record, and not likely to be beaten for a long time. Liddell's own comment on these two races was 'I think I could do better if I trained for them'.
>
> A man who can improve on 47.8 for the 400 is a marvel. Knowing Liddell as I do, it can be taken for granted that his comment was not a boast, but merely an honest statement of fact. He is a non-smoker and does not drink, but it may be easily understood that however good his normal condition, special training would have given him that extra edge so necessary for Olympic standard. My own opinion is that Liddell is still the best quarter-miler in the world.

Liddell was then not yet twenty-seven years old. That same year he ran in the South Manchurian Railway celebrations for the coronation of the Emperor of Japan. The Japanese and the French Olympic teams were there, their laurels fresh from Amsterdam. 'And it happened, somehow, that I won the 200 and the 400 metres,' Eric told an interviewer a year or two later, underplaying everything as usual.

That interview, conducted while Eric was on furlough in Canada in 1932, is a good example of the ability to deflate pomposity which Eric had practised at primary school and been perfecting ever since. The interviewer, R.E. Knowles, asked in an excessively long-winded way how long he had been a missionary when his race at the railway celebrations came to pass.

'Just three years,' said Eric.

'And was there any moaning at the bar?'

'What bar?' murmured Eric.

'The bar of public, religious and clerical opinion. Did the missionary authorities instruct you to moderate your pace?'

'Oh no.'

'Had you had their permission to compete?'

'Oh no.'

'Do you think your pedal prowess is a help to you in your work?' continued the metaphor-struck Mr Knowles indefatigably.

'Sure.'

'Do you ever preach from the text "So run that ye may obtain"?'

'No, I'd sooner preach on "The race is not to the swift",' replied Eric, enjoying himself hugely.

Mr Knowles pressed on, and his persistence was rewarded by the nearest anyone ever came to information from Eric about his sporting successes.

'When was your last big race, Mr Liddell?'

'In 1929, I think. I raced the great German runner, Dr Otto Peltzer, holder of the world's 500 metres record, also of the record for the half-mile, also for 1500 metres.'

'And how did you come out?'

'Oh, I won the 400 metres. Peltzer won the 800.'

'And have you ever raced since?'

'Well, now that you speak of it, I believe I did. I believe I won the North China championship in 1930, but that was all.'

What the relentless Mr Knowles did not manage to elicit from Eric was that, after the race with Peltzer, the German had said to him in the pavilion in his broken English:

'You represent Britain at the next Olympic Games?'

'No, I'm too old,' Eric replied.

'How old?'

'Twenty-eight.'

Otto Peltzer roared with laughter. 'Too old? I am thirty-two, and will represent Germany at the next Games in 1932.'

Then, according to the former Royal Scots runner who told the story, Peltzer said, 'You train for 800 metres, and you are the greatest man in the world at that distance.' Peltzer was the world record-holder for the same distance.

As Liddell had acknowledged to the arch R.E. Knowles, the race against the world 500-metre champion Otto Pelzer was his last major running competition. The Amateur Athletic Association award he won in Tientsin that day was to be his final gold medal. More than sixty years later, in June 1991, Liddell's three daughters gave this medal to the school in what is now Tianjin where Eric taught for so many happy years. It was presented on behalf of the family by David Michell, whom Liddell befriended in the Japanese internment camp towards the end of his life. Michell was on his way to a ceremony at Weifang to dedicate a memorial stone near the site of Eric's grave. The gold medal he handed over at the school that June day in 1991 had Eric Liddell's name on the back and on the other side the words 'Tientsin AAA' with an inscription in Latin which Michell translated to the assembled Chinese audience as 'Harmony among nations'. On the family's behalf, he said, he was presenting it to the school with much emotion.

Eric's Olympic medals were handed over to Edinburgh University the following year. On 20 May 1992 his eldest daughter, now Mrs Patricia Russell, presented them to HRH the Duke of Edinburgh, vice-chancellor of the university, at a small ceremony in the Playfair Library Hall.

While Eric Liddell's sporting triumphs in China mounted, his unorthodox running style was turning as many heads in Tientsin as it had in Craiglockart. Indeed, on one occasion it was more than heads he turned as he flew along the racetrack doing the 100 metres and knocked a photographer for six. Watching from the seats around the arena were his brother Rob and the matron of his hospital from the village of Siaochang, who had wobbled and bumped along the long dirt track on the first motorcycle ever seen in Siaochang.

The matron, Annie Buchan, recalled the occasion vividly:

> I will never forget Eric coming along with his head back and just tearing along. A Chinese photographer, not realising the speed Eric was travelling at, came right into Eric's path with his tripod. Of course Eric came right into him. The photographer went flying, and the tripod too, and Eric fell flat on his face. Rob and I rushed down. Eric was just lying there, and we carried him into a tent unconscious. When he came round, all he said was, 'I was just winded.'

Another race that has become part of the Liddell legend, so much so that it even featured in a strip cartoon in the British *Victor* comic for boys, was his celebrated 'boat-race' leap. This was the jump that really made the 'Flying Scotsman' label stick. Liddell was running at an athletics contest at Darien in 1928. His last race, the 400 metres, was being run just half an hour before the boat to Manchuria was due to sail. He had to catch that boat. It was twenty minutes from the racetrack to the boat, so he ordered a taxi to wait near the finishing tape.

Along he thundered, breaking the finishing tape in first place. Hardly slackening pace, he made straight for the taxi. Suddenly 'God Save the King' rent the air and he slithered to a halt. Straight as a post he stood there, the taxi a few yards away. 'G-o-d save the King,' they ended, and he made a lurch for the taxi. But the band then struck up the 'Marseillaise' in tribute to the Frenchman who had come second. So there he was, stuck rigid again.

'The taxi made it in great time,' he recounted later:

> I took a healthy hop, step and leap, and was on the edge of the wharf before it stopped. The boat was steadily moving out − too far to jump. But a bit of a tidal wave threw it back a little. Then I flung my bags and jumped. I tried to remember in the very act how a gazelle jumps. I felt like one, and I made it. Just made it.

A newspaper correspondent in the car said Eric covered fifteen feet of water. Eric himself, playing it down, said it was less. But legend has credited the Flying Scotsman with a fifteen-foot leap all the same.

The pleasure Eric derived from running, in China as much as in Britain, and the obvious continued thrill of competition, make one wonder if he ever regretted the lost opportunity of making sport his life. Did he mind missing the 1928 Olympics? What did he feel when Otto Peltzer told him he could be the world's greatest at 800 metres? When he was supervising the chemistry class, or in later years tramping the steamy Siaochang countryside with nothing to eat, did he ever wish he had devoted himself to the sport that was his pleasure?

The redoubtable R.E. Knowles asked him much the same in the Toronto interview. Phrased in Mr Knowles' inimitable style, the question was: 'Are you glad you gave your life to missionary work? Don't you miss the limelight, the rush, the frenzy, the cheers, the rich red wine of victory?'

And Eric's answer was this: 'Oh well, of course it's natural for a chap to think over all that sometimes, but I'm glad I'm at the work I'm engaged in now. A fellow's life counts for far more at this than the other. Not a corruptible crown, but an incorruptible, you know.'

He used to tell his wife he was born lazy and all sports came so easily that he would have been content to make a living from billiards, at which he was a dab hand. 'I think at one time he would very much like to have made sports his career,' Florence said. 'He did say he would have been quite happy to live by his wits in some kind of sport. But that was before he met D.P. Thomson.'

The meeting at Armadale really had changed his life. He still liked the same things: the lick of the wind on his face as he ran, the joy of breaking the tape at the winning line, the satisfaction of being the best at something and knowing it. But he needed more, and once he had made up his mind that it was so, he simply surrendered his life to the God to whom he had committed his life. It was a willing surrender, an unforced obedience, which gave Liddell both a serene confidence and a genuine humility. These were the qualities which had the most profound effect on those who knew him.

Early in 1929, James Liddell suffered a slight stroke and was encouraged to return to Scotland to recuperate. Eric accompanied his father, his mother Mary, Jenny and Ernest, to Taku (now Tangu) to catch the boat to Rotterdam and thence home. At the age of fifty-eight James was hoping to return to missionary service after he had recovered, but his health declined further in Scotland and he never saw China again.

After his family's departure, Eric moved out of No. 6 London Mission and into a bachelor flat at the college. The men with whom he shared it later talked about their months in the Tientsin flat as the richest of their lives. One of them, the surgeon George Dorling said of him: 'We three were miles below the standard Eric set for himself. But he was always our friend. I knew that every time I could count on Eric. Nothing ever shocked him. His love was too great to be shocked.'

Another flatmate, Scotsman David McGavin, described him as 'a perfect Christian gentleman'. The eulogies are endless:

'I never heard Eric say an unkind word of anyone,' said another.

'Eric was the most Christ-like man I knew.'

'Eric had a great sense of humour, but if work had to be done, that came first.'

Someone once spotted a fly on a biscuit when they were being entertained to coffee and, mindful of the danger of germs, warned Eric not to touch it. 'But this was the biscuit that Eric was careful to take,' says the storyteller. 'His action was not intended as a rebuke to me – that would never occur to him – but to make certain that no one else should suffer discomfort as a result of eating a biscuit defiled by the fly.'

Of course, these were the tributes of men to whom words like 'Christ-like' and 'Christian gentleman' were everyday language, and whose own lives were dedicated to the attainment of the kind of qualities they saw in Eric Liddell. They spoke in a more fulsome way than we are used to today, and it is always tempting to sanctify a good man when he is dead. All the same, they point to a remarkably attractive character.

Liddell seemed to draw his strength, self-discipline and air of quiet serenity from his early-morning sessions of prayer, meditation and Bible

Eric's sister, Jenny.

study. He would come out from that and stride through the rest of the day as though the Sermon on the Mount were still ringing in his ears. Whatever it was that he received in those morning sessions he spent the rest of the day giving out to others. He measured his standards by it, and if he thought those standards had slipped, he was as stern with himself as he declined to be with others. Somewhere in this daily discipline of faith lay the secret of the man, and perhaps the secret of how he ran.

David McGavin once asked him if he ever prayed that he would win a race. He replied, 'No, I have never prayed that I would win a race. I have, of course, prayed about the athletic meetings, asking that in this, too, God might be glorified.'

The young girl he was about to start courting said years later:

> He believed in praying. One hour every morning it was. I tried to keep up with him but, boy, I was away behind him. I think that was the secret of his life. He would think through the whole day and what he had to do, and that was where he would get the strength to do it.

He was never too busy to see the Chinese students who called on him, day or night, and never too pious to lark about with the youngsters ('He had a touch of devilry in him,' said one later). If there was mischief afoot, he was usually in the vanguard. 'How could you behave like that when you were with Mr Liddell?' scandalised mothers would scold, little dreaming that Mr Liddell had been in the thick of it.

His sense of humour defused many a conflict among the missionaries. In the missionary compound tensions and quarrels were as rife as they always are when strong-minded people are living close together. 'Oh, the missionaries were very stuffed shirts,' said the son of a missionary who was then at Tientsin Grammar School with Eric's brother, Ernest, and future sweetheart, Florence. 'Especially the evangelicals. They felt they were God's chosen people and that others were letting them down all the time and dropping moral standards. Eric wasn't like that. He could live on both sides.'

But he would let no one walk over him. There was a determined streak in Eric Liddell never far from the surface, whether he was refusing to run on a Sunday or, as he was about to do, choosing a bride.

7

'I Didn't Even Know He Was Courting'

When Eric Liddell told his friends in July 1930 that he was engaged to be married, they were flabbergasted. 'I didn't even know he was courting,' said his close friend, Bob Knight, whose ship was in Tientsin harbour at the time.

Even the girl in question had not been aware that Eric had romantic intentions towards her. She was only seventeen at the time, ten years younger than him. Her name was Florence McKenzie, the daughter of Canadian missionaries whom Eric had known for years. She had been in Eric's brother Ernest's class at school and she played the piano in the Union Church Sunday school, where Eric was superintendent and where she had once been a pupil.

'I was terribly naïve,' she explained. 'Eric had become such a part of the family that I just didn't notice anything. Of course I was desperately in love with him, but I just couldn't get over the fact that he wanted to marry me.'

But tea-drinkers in a popular Tientsin café called Kiesslings had begun to suspect; and friends of Florence had guessed weeks before. Eric had always taken an interest in young people, but this was ridiculous. He was showing a remarkable enthusiasm for taking whole gangs of them on picnics, for walks, or for tea at Kiesslings. But according to the rules of their tight society, a man could not just ask a girl to go out with him, especially if she was only seventeen and just out of school. Subtlety was called for. So observing the conventions but also sending them up with his usual aplomb, Eric simply invited Florence's whole circle of friends and classmates along whenever he wanted to take her out. Tennis parties at the Pei-tai-ho beach resort helped, too, while the McKenzies were becoming used to Eric materialising at their front door, breezily suggesting that the entire family come for a walk in the summer rain.

Eric's wife-to-be, Florence, when she was a schoolgirl in China.

Florence was planning to go to Canada to train as a nurse, but she was so upset at failing a French exam she needed for entry into the hospital that she talked about giving up the whole idea. It was then that Eric spoke up. Not for one minute must she think of giving up, he said. And, by the way, would she like to come out for a walk, because there was something he wanted to ask her?

'When he proposed to me I really was quite stunned,' Florence remembered. 'I said, "Are you sure you really mean it?" And he said yes, he did really mean it. There were several other girls of his own age, and I thought, they're just going to kill me.' She laughed, a merry, throaty chuckle.

'I accepted him right away,' she added, her mass of black, curly hair grey in her seventies but her rich Canadian accent still bubbling with the vivacity that Eric loved her for. She was a bright, happy girl, with the same uncomplicated approach to life as Eric. Quiet but sunny-natured, she had a down-to-earth quality and strength of mind which showed at once in her conversation all those years later. This was not the kind of woman to have had much time for excessive piety. She laughed:

> I can't stand these people who are so goody-goody and holy-holy. They bring out the worst in me and make me want to go the opposite way. Eric wasn't like that. His wonderful sense of humour saved him from ever being like that. He had a poker-faced humour, and you had to watch his eyes very carefully. They usually gave him away, if you looked closely.

People often mention Eric Liddell's eyes. When he was at school, teachers soon learned that the only way to catch him out was to read his eyes. And he needed some catching-out as a youngster. His chief characteristic, which remained the main weapon in the Liddell armoury, was a look of such cherubic innocence that he was usually the last to be suspected of the schoolboy pranks he instigated.

'Liddell,' the headmaster told him once in class, in a sudden burst of enlightenment, 'I am beginning to think you are not as good as you look.' And he wasn't. But he had a smile that seldom failed to get him out of trouble. This instinctive ability to disarm opposition always served Eric well. He got his own way with such quiet charm that people hardly noticed they were giving way. He scandalised his mother once by walking the streets of douce Edinburgh in a lurid shirt he had bought in Hawaii. 'Eric, you can't go out in that!' she wailed; but Eric, who loved wild colours and didn't care what the neighbours thought of his shirt, just grinned and wore it. 'He knew what he wanted,' says Florence. 'He was very sweet with his mother, but he just went his own way.'

When Florence accepted his proposal that day in Tientsin, Eric immediately sent home for a diamond ring. He wanted one with five diamonds in a row, the same as his mother's. So his mother and sister went to a jeweller's in Edinburgh and bought a ring, which they sent to China. As soon as it arrived, he and Florence became officially engaged. It was to be a long engagement, like his parents' had been. Florence left soon afterwards to do her nurse's training in Canada, and it was four years before they married in Tientsin in 1934.

Meanwhile, Eric went home on his first furlough to Scotland. After a stay in Toronto with his fiancée and her family, he arrived back in

Edinburgh in the summer of 1931. His parents were now finally settled in Scotland's capital after James Liddell's enforced retirement from mission work due to continuing ill health.

It was now seven years since Eric had won his gold medal at the Paris Olympics, six years since his *annus mirabilis* of evangelistic speaking up and down the country. But Scotland had not forgotten him. He was immediately swooped on by the sporting world, the religious world, the temperance world and the newspapers. His welcome back was tumultuous. For thousands of people in Scotland, the Olympic champion turned missionary was still a national hero.

His formal purpose in returning was to take a course of studies at the Scottish Congregational College in Edinburgh with a view to being ordained; but so great was the demand to see and hear him speak that a college committee had to be set up to coordinate his schedule. He spoke wherever he was called: at sporting rallies all over Scotland, and from pulpits in churches of all denominations, not just in Scotland but in England and Northern Ireland as well. At a great 'Public Welcome Home Meeting' in Edinburgh, attended by leading churchmen and sporting luminaries like G.P.S. Macpherson, the Scottish rugby captain, Liddell set the uncompromising tone of all the speeches that were to follow:

> We are all missionaries. We carry our religion with us, or we allow our religion to carry us. Wherever we go, we either bring people nearer to Christ, or we repel them from Christ. We are working for the great Kingdom of God – the time when all people will turn to Christ as their Leader – and will not be afraid to own him as such.

Apart from the evangelism, he could not avoid talking about the current political situation in China, about which so much had been written in the press in the preceding months. To meeting after meeting he tried to explain the growth of patriotic nationalism in China and the Chinese hostility towards foreigners, even towards the missionaries who were working there in a spirit of selflessness. He took his message about Chinese nationalism to a short series of packed meetings in Belfast, a brave thing to do in the political climate of Northern Ireland at the time:

> In a city such as Tientsin there are colleges in what are termed the concessions, areas taken over by foreign powers. Chinese public opinion, strengthened by a growing national feeling that other nations had taken

from her what should be hers, has been asking that these concessions should be given back.

I don't want to go into the political aspect of the question, not being a politician myself. But just glancing at the matter I feel it would be extremely difficult to give this land back immediately. But our policy – and the people in Tientsin are trying to do it – is gradually to hand it over. I think that this method will not only cause less complication between nation and nation, but is the most Christ-like way in which it can be done.

One large rally in Edinburgh that must have pleased him was held by the Lord's Day Observance Society of Scotland. Here Eric Liddell moved a resolution that was seconded by a young minister, a future moderator of the General Assembly of the Church of Scotland called Leonard Small, then newly ordained to St John's Church, Bathgate. The resolution, which was carried unanimously, declared:

That the meeting is of the opinion that the increasing use of the Lord's Day for games and recreations, however harmless in themselves, is detrimental to the highest interest of the youth of the country, as well as adding to the amount of unnecessary labour of other people; and calls on all young people's organisations to give full consideration to this aspect of the question.

Eric Liddell's unbreakable stand on the principle of Sunday observance at the Paris Olympics had been no flash in the pan. He was to stand by it all his life, even in the Japanese internment camp in China where he was to pass his last months, and where he was responsible for all sporting and recreational activities. There was only one occasion on which he broke the Sabbath there, but that story comes later.

In June 1932, Eric Liddell was ordained to the ministry in the chapel of the Scottish Congregational Church. His furlough was now over and it was as the Revd Eric Liddell that he set off for China. He travelled by way of Canada, so that he could visit his fiancée in Toronto. Florence was by then in the middle of her training course at the Toronto General Hospital. In Toronto he also met the British Olympics athletics team, who had stopped off for some training on their way to the 1932 Olympics at Los Angeles.

It was there that he also met that egregious newspaperman Mr R.E. Knowles. The tone and prominent display of the interview he published shows something of the extent of Liddell's world fame at that time. The article concluded with a coy aside from Mr Knowles to all the Canadian women who must be simply dying to know why Eric was lingering in Toronto, hardly the most direct route from Britain to China. For these women, he wrote, 'who would not smile again for a week if I stopped right here, I have been permitted to say that a certain missionary-ess, a nurse in training at Toronto General Hospital… is the occasion of Mr Eric Liddell's divine detour.'

Eric escaped back to Tientsin, where he was due to resume work at the Anglo-Chinese College at the start of September. He now had extra responsibilities: in addition to being superintendent of the Union Church Sunday School, he took over as secretary of the college and chairman of the Games Committee, and was put in charge of the religious activities of the college. Life at the college was changing: there had been no more strikes, but since Dr Lavington Hart retired in 1930, there had been a succession of Chinese principals, and relations were sometimes uneasy.

Outside the college, with its daily round of teaching and studying and its beach parties at Pei-tai-ho, a vicious civil war was being waged between the Communist Red Army and the Nationalists under Chiang Kai-shek for the control of China's political soul. There were massacres, burnings and lootings all over the country. In 1931, Japan invaded Manchuria in north-eastern China on a trumped-up pretext; in the following year they launched a savage assault on Shanghai, then as now the largest and busiest port in the Far East. Despite the gallant defence put up by Chiang Kai-shek's Nineteenth Route Army, large parts of Shanghai were flattened by carrier-bombers and naval gunfire before Britain stepped in to arrange a ceasefire.

Tientsin itself was unaffected by the strife to the north and south of it, and the college carried on as usual. The only recorded reaction from Eric Liddell is in a letter he wrote after one of his classes was ordered by the government to take up military drill: 'Although I hate war, and feel the attitude of Christian people to it is going to be one of the greatest challenges in the future, yet it has smartened up some of the lads quite a bit.'

During this period, Eric was preoccupied with his personal affairs. His sister Jenny was now happily married to an Edinburgh widower, Dr Charles Somerville, but his father, who had been such an inspiration to him always, died in the autumn of 1933. Eric wrote a stream of comforting, affectionate letters to his bereaved mother:

Wedding photograph
of Eric and Florence,
1934, at the Union
Church, Tientsin.

When this letter reaches you near the end of February the first flowers
of spring should be starting up. Surely by then the snowdrops should be
out, and a little later will come the crocuses and daffodils. Jenny's garden
will soon begin to bloom again. You must go out there, Mother, and stay
with her, especially at that time of year. I am glad that I have recently had
a furlough and been with you, for now I can picture it all so clearly and
seem to know what you are doing.

At the same time he was having his house in Tientsin redecorated for
his wedding, which was planned for the spring of the following year,
1934. Florence passed all her nursing exams in Toronto that winter, and
left for China at the beginning of February. Five weeks later she was
at Tientsin, and on 27 March 1934 they were married in the Union
Church there.

The front-page report in the *Tientsin and Peking Times and North China News* is splendidly flowery, equal to the British press reports of any 1930s society wedding in London or Edinburgh:

> There was a large attendance of foreigners and Chinese at the Union Church this afternoon when the Rev. Eric H. Liddell, the well-known Olympic champion, was united in matrimony with Miss Florence Jean McKenzie, the daughter of Mr and Mrs Hugh McKenzie, well known and much respected residents of Tientsin. Prior to this the civil ceremony took place this morning at HBM Consulate before M.S.G. Beare, HBM Consul.
>
> The nuptial knot was tied by Rev. Eric Richards (Minister of Union Church) assisted by Dr Murdoch McKenzie, who, besides having been a resident in China for the past forty-three years, also christened the bride. To the strains of Lohengrin's Wedding March the bride entered on the arm of her father who gave her away.
>
> The bride's wedding dress, which was also her mother's wedding dress, was of white satin with lace veil trimmed with a sprig of orange blossoms, and she carried a bouquet of pink carnations. The lace veil had also been worn by Miss Liddell, the sister of the bridegroom, at her own wedding. The bride was attended by Miss Gwyneth Rees as bridesmaid, who was charmingly gowned in green silk lace with green hat to match and she carried a bouquet of pink carnations.
>
> The best man was Dr George Dorling, and the ushers Mr Gerald Luxon, Mr R. Schmuser, and Mr E.S. Box. Mrs Hugh McKenzie, the bride's mother, wore a black georgette dress, trimmed with lace, with black hat to match, and she carried a bouquet of pink carnations. The church was artistically decorated for the occasion with flowers and plants by Mrs Gerald Luxon and Mrs C.H.B. Longman. Mr C.W.W. Lewis officiated at the organ.
>
> After the religious ceremony a reception was held at the home of the bride's parents, No. 70 Cambridge Road, and was attended by a large number of the many friends of the happy couple. The guests were received under a large silver bell covered with ferns and pink carnations. Dr Murdoch McKenzie proposed the health of the bride and bride groom, which was suitably responded to by the bride. [It was actually Eric who replied to the toast.]

Eric, who, like most missionaries' children, had spent much of his childhood and youth separated from his parents, slipped easily and joyfully into family life. Two daughters came along in quick succession, first Patricia, and then Heather. When Heather was born, there was the usual family debate over a name for the baby. Eric offered to solve the problem by putting two pieces of paper in a hat, one with Flo's final choice, one with his. With great solemnity he drew out a paper with the name 'Heather' on it, his own choice. It was only later that he confessed he had written 'Heather' on both bits of paper. It says much for Florence's sense of humour that she accepted the decision, and much for the quality of their marriage. They laughed a great deal and shared everything.

Eric was a typically proud father. His children were simply the most perfect creatures that had ever been born on this earth. He adored them. His letters home to Scotland were full of momentous details like the first teeth, the first steps, the first falls, the sleeping averages. It is interesting to note his athlete's way of describing baby Patricia's progress in walking: not 'She took so-and-so many steps today', or 'She made it right across the room', but 'She did twelve yards on her own'.

Their family life was a happy one, although Eric's work led to increasing absences. When he was at home they particularly loved going on bicycle rides together, Patricia on a small seat on the crossbar of her father's bike, Heather in the basket at Flo's handlebars. Of that marriage, which was to last only eleven years, Florence would write to D.P. Thomson:

> I will always thank God that I had the rare privilege of being Eric's wife. I think we had more fun and happiness in our eleven years together than lots of couples have in a whole lifetime of married life. He was a perfectly grand husband and so sweet with the children. Patricia, the eldest, has vivid memories of him, but unfortunately Heather's memories aren't quite so vivid, because ever since she was ten months old, Eric was never with us more than six weeks at one stretch.

Not only did Eric Liddell see little of his second daughter, Heather, he never saw his third daughter, Maureen, at all, for the time was coming when China's seething military turmoil would split the family up for ever.

The first challenge to the Liddells' cosy domestic bliss arrived in the spring of 1935, barely a year after their marriage, but it came less from the political situation in China than from the internal politics of the London Missionary Society. There was a shortage of missionaries in the countryside, and the Tientsin Anglo-Chinese College was thought by some to be appropriating an unfairly large share of the available staff. Eric was asked by the district council if he would agree to go and help with the work at Siaochang, where he had been born and raised and where his older brother, Rob, was already working as a missionary doctor.

It was a dismaying prospect for a newly married couple with an infant daughter. Siaochang was in an area devastated by war and drought. It was desperately in need of help but, on the other hand, moving from Tientsin would mean breaking up the family, for Eric would have to be away for months on end. It would also mean leaving classes of intelligent young students to work among illiterate peasants and, of course, the end of convivial tennis parties and teas at Kiesslings. Besides, as Eric and Flo reminded each other in their many heart-searching discussions, Eric's Chinese was still barely fluent, and he would have considerable difficulty in communicating with the unlettered souls in his care.

It was a difficult choice for a young couple to have to face, and at first they decided that the move would not be a good idea. In his annual report to headquarters in London, Eric wrote:

> The summer brought me face to face with the question as to whether I felt called to country work, seeing that that section of the work was so understaffed. I thought over it then, and have been thinking over it ever since, and cannot but feel that I am more equipped for educational work, both by training and temperament. Besides, at the present time it would make it extremely difficult in the college to reduce numbers.

But gradually, inexorably, the pressure built up: economic pressure on the London Missionary Society but also the private pressure of Eric's own conscience. In 1936, the district council decided that Eric should be released from the college for four months to explore 'country work' at first hand. By the beginning of 1937, his mind was made up. He would go.

Eric Liddell was no martyr to asceticism: he liked the good things of life and had an easygoing nature, with no particular relish for changes or difficulties for their own sake. Life was going fine, thank you: an adored young wife, two adored young daughters, a satisfying job, comfortable lifestyle. His colleagues at the college urged him to stay on at Tientsin, saying that he was badly needed there, and Eric tried hard to believe them. But, in the end he decided, after much prayer, that it was his duty to go.

Florence Liddell was later to write to D.P. Thomson:

It was a big step, involving many changes, and it took him a long time to be sure he was doing the right thing. There were friends on both sides of the question who felt very strongly about it. However, after much prayerful consideration of all the points involved, he felt God was calling him to the country, and I think it was quite obvious he did the right thing. He loved the work, his health improved, and I think he blossomed out in a new way.

A missionary community, once convinced that one of their number is on the wrong track, can be a formidable force to be reckoned with. Eric was made to feel all the weight of their disapproval at what they considered his foolhardiness in throwing away his vital educational work in the big city. 'It really hurt him,' said Florence, 'but he never let on. That was one place where I learned that he could take criticism.'

Nothing would shake Eric's resolve once he had decided on his course. In December 1937 he left Tientsin to join his brother Rob in Siaochang. The wheel was coming full circle.

8

'It is Wonderful to Feel at One with the People'

Imagine Siaochang in the 1930s. It is a village in the heart of the Great North Plain in southern Hopei. The fields lie ruined by drought, locusts and the depredations of marauding soldiers. Big families are squashed into tiny houses; hunger or disease is in nearly every home. These are simple people who cannot read but love to learn. They are frightened people who know that their next meal, even perhaps their lives, may depend on which Japanese soldier, or Chinese guerrilla, or wandering bandit may pass through next. They are slow-moving, farming people who are having it hard.

Here was a China unchanged by the centuries. There were still girls whose feet were bound, crushed and maimed from the age of five, with the toes tucked under the sole. The damp cotton bandages were changed every day, the feet massaged and bound again, to make these feet grow unnaturally small. No respectable man wanted to marry a girl unless her feet were bound. With unbound feet, she would rank as a slave girl. But in the countryside around Siaochang every peasant was a slave, to feudal lords, to war, hunger, drought and disease. Faithfully they appealed to their many gods. One was the kitchen god, with its image pasted on the wall. Every New Year the picture of the kitchen god was changed for a new one; the old picture was then burned, but only after the god's mouth had been smeared with sugar, to make sure that it could only say sweet words when it reported the family's behaviour to the authorities in heaven.

On the night of 7 July 1937, a few months before Eric Liddell's arrival at Siaochang Mission, Japan launched a full-scale invasion of China following a minor military incident at the Marco Polo Bridge west of Peking. The Japanese had been encroaching on Chinese territory for years, greatly helped by Chiang Kai-shek's obsession with fighting his Communist rivals. In his preoccupation he ignored not only the invader

but the appalling plight of the peasantry in North China, whose liveli-
hood was withering in droughts or being washed away in the floods
that afflicted the north in the 1930s.

Encouraged by the submissive attitude of the preoccupied Nationalists,
the Japanese penetration of North China continued, heading for
Chungking (Chongqing) on the Yangtse River. Eventually, in August
1937, the Nationalists and the Communists joined forces in an anti-
Japanese United Front, a reluctant and short-lived cooperation. The
main body of the Red Army stationed in the north-west was reorganised
into the Eighth Route Army of the National Revolutionary Army, and
an extensive guerrilla campaign against the Japanese-held railways swung
into action. The people of the Siaochang district were to learn all about
the Eighth Route Army in the days to come, as the fortunes of battle
swayed this way and that.

The Japanese campaign against the Chinese was fierce, and designed
to humiliate. They adopted blitzkrieg bombing and terror tactics to
encourage quick surrender. By the end of 1939, the year in which the
Second World War started for the Western world, Japan would control
the main lines of communication and the major cities of eastern China,
such as Shanghai, Tientsin and Peking itself. But they failed to dominate
the rural areas, and at about the time when Eric Liddell moved into
the country areas, Chinese guerrilla units were beginning to operate
behind enemy lines. Whenever they attacked a blockhouse or blew up
an ammunition train, the Japanese took immediate reprisals against the
civilian population.

The people of Siaochang were right in the middle of these assaults and
counter-assaults. The two main railway routes, from Tientsin to Shanghai
and from Peking to Hankow, passed within forty miles to the east and
fifty miles to the west of Siaochang. The railway lines were in the hands
of the Japanese, but the land in between was controlled by the Chinese.
The fighting was interminable, and the people in the district looked to
the missionaries for protection. The mission compound at Siaochang
had a hospital, which was always crowded out, and a church with refuge
for 500, where the women and children hid during attacks. There was
also a big girls' school, for it was only in the missions that girls could be
educated at all in China at that time.

The church, school and living quarters were inside the mud wall
which surrounded the compound. Over the front gate a sign read:
'Chung, Wai, I Chai': 'Chinese and Foreigners, All One Home'. The
Chinese had put up the sign when the buildings had had to be rebuilt

after their destruction in the Boxer Rising, the conflagration which had sent Eric's parents fleeing from their first mission post in 1901.

Siaochang was the centre of a wide field of activity covered by the London Missionary Society on the Great Plain. It was a district the size of Wales, and Eric was expected to cover it as an itinerant evangelist, visiting churches, advising the Chinese preachers, sharing the lives of the people he visited, answering their questions, dealing with their problems. He needed all his celebrated patience for the job. The dreary treks on foot or by bicycle across miles of either parched or flooded land were enough to sap the strength and weary the spirit, without having to dodge bandits and guerrillas and explain his business to a succession of Japanese gun-barrels. Outdoor preaching meant soakings or scorchings, depending on the season. When he stayed in villages, he went hungry if his host did, and slept on the floor and shared the misery of those who shared their roof with him. Sometimes he found villages burned out, the menfolk shot dead, their families numb with grief.

The sufferings of this area had started years before the Japanese moved in, when civil war was raging and anti-Christian feeling was at its height. While Eric was teaching chemistry in Tientsin, the missionaries of Siaochang were already in the thick of the strife that was convulsing the land. In a booklet called *Adventure in Faith* Annie Buchan, the Scottish matron of the hospital, described the perils they had faced in 1927 which were now being repeated ten years later:

In the spring of 1927 we had a message from the British Consul ordering us to evacuate for Tientsin without delay. We had no choice. After consulting our Chinese colleagues we set off with a heavy heart; but, fortunately, after an absence of five months we were allowed to return...

There came another order to evacuate in May 1928. Anti-foreign feeling had been stirred up, and we were in a country station a long way from the railway. It was considered advisable for us to get out while it was still possible. This time, however, we were rebellious. We wanted to take the risk, but the Chinese warned that the uprising was serious. They advised us to go. Saying goodbye was unforgettable. One well-meaning friend said, 'You are fortunate. The British Consul will take care of you. We have no one to protect us, we have to depend on God.' It is not difficult to imagine how we felt leaving our dear friends in this way to face whatever was to come.

Unforgettable also was the five-day journey travelling zig-zag across the Plain, avoiding known routes in fear of meeting soldiers, or being caught between the opposing armies. There were also renegade soldiers on the rampage, plundering for money in order to help them escape from either army. Our transport was the usual mission springless cart, with the Rev. W.F. Rowlands in charge of us women. Mrs C. Busby stayed behind: someone had to stay, as the compound was full of refugees.

We had not gone far when our carter took fright and refused to go any farther. Suddenly, soldiers seemed to be springing from nowhere, demanding our mules. One soldier covered us with his gun while another unharnessed the mules. After pleading, and finally giving some money, they left us with one mule, the least able to carry our load. Our carter saw that it was as dangerous at that stage to return as to move forward, so we moved on. But, where could we stay the night? Soldiers were on the march all around us. Each village we came to seemed lifeless. Not a soul to be seen. Not a sound except, now and then, the cry or whimper of a baby.

To our delight, at one village we saw the sign of a Methodist Mission. When we knocked, a man opened the door, just a slit, and whispered that everyone had left. He was obviously scared to let us in but, being desperate, we pushed our way inside. To our surprise there were more Chinese within hiding from the soldiers. One man had been a patient in our hospital and knew Mr Rowlands who had baptised him five years earlier. His name was Mr Han, and he did everything for our comfort as far as possible within a stripped building. We ourselves were safely indoors, but what about our cart? The mule was brought in, and the cart dismantled and brought under roof, for fear of the soldiers!

It had been blowing a dust storm, and we were very grimy, and very tired. Pastor Han and Pastor Hu pleaded with us to stay and hide with them; but, as in many a tight corner, we prayed for guidance and felt assured that we should press on regardless of danger. We lay down as we were, in our clothes, ready to start at daylight.

Being already dressed, and there being no water to wash, we did not delay. A cup of tea was brought to us and, after the cart had been made ready, we were off. The weather was unusual. We had been through a dust storm, and now it was heavy, blinding rain with head wind. The carter was not in a good mood. He turned and saw me shivering, my teeth chattering with the cold. 'God isn't favouring you now,' he said. But the bad weather was in our favour and we were not molested, although we had not gone far when we met a band of soldiers. They spoke to us, and when they knew we had come from the Jesus Mission at Siaochang they were friendly and sang hymns. Other soldiers passed us in a hurry to go on.

We had been told of how soldiers plundered the poor village people, and now we were seeing them at work – kicking open doors, pushing their swords through them – and heard the cries of the terrified people inside. There was, of course, nothing to plunder from us, but once again we felt ashamed to go free. The band of soldiers were also ashamed for us to see what their fellow soldiers were doing and offered to escort us. We did not want that, however, knowing that we would be safer on our own.

Very soon another band of soldiers caught up on us. They blamed us for having a bodyguard and for breaking Treaty Rights. Finally, they all came along with us, making us walk while they took it in turn to ride upon the cart. Things were looking ugly. We were willing to walk but were not happy about the uneasy peace. Fortunately for us, the enemy was on their tail and they ran off in front as fast as they could.

For the missionaries of Siaochang at that time life seemed to be a succession of alarms and excursions. The civil war continued to disrupt their work, even before the Japanese moved in:

One day a general of one of the Chinese armies arrived with his soldiers, a man of both wealth and power, and a number of wives and concubines. I escorted him round the hospital and his eyes filled with tears at the sight of so many babies ill and starving. Because of the civil war, I explained, we could not get milk, which could be more nourishing than the local bean curd milk. Nothing was said, but, a few days later, a number of cases of tinned milk arrived, a gift from the general, a man who had no use for religion and was hardened at the sight of blood on the battlefield. What could have happened to have stirred and softened his heart, at the sight of babies starving from lack of nourishment? I don't know, but he never had another opportunity of doing a good deed for, shortly afterwards, his army was defeated and he himself murdered about a mile from Siaochang.

Around this time Eric's brother Rob and his wife and daughter joined Annie Buchan and the hospital staff at Siaochang. Rob Liddell had trained at Edinburgh University as a doctor and good doctors were worth their weight in gold at Siaochang, where the mission hospital had over a hundred beds and was expanding all the time. Although the hospital had a well-established baby clinic, the rate of infant mortality was astounding. A frightening number of babies died from convulsions in the first few weeks of life, mainly through tetanus. The most common method of post-natal care of the newborn infant was to fill a piece of rag with earth from the ground and wrap it round the umbilical cord: the baby was then laid aside unwashed.

The Chinese had no cows' milk, and rice water was not sufficient for baby feeding; the mothers, who spent much of their time working in the fields, seldom had sufficient milk themselves. Tinned milk was unavailable. To offset this deficiency the mission hospital started a soya-bean milk kitchen, where beans were crushed and prepared with the necessary addition of calcium and sugar. Midwifery was still hazardous, and full of surprises. Annie Buchan admitted a woman who was ill with a supposed abdominal tumour and was taken into the operating theatre for examination: 'She promptly gave birth to four baby boys, one after the other. Sadly, all had been dead for some time.'

The medical superintendent of the hospital was Dr Kenneth McCall, who had been at school with Eric and knew him well. He was delighted at Eric's decision to leave his safe job in Tientsin and join the work at Siaochang. But he was keenly aware of the perils facing a wandering country evangelist. The missionaries were all vulnerable targets in an area in which as many as nine different armies were fighting each other. As Britons, they were suspected by the Japanese of spying and as Christians their presence was at best merely tolerated by the Chinese Communists because they needed the hospital for their wounded. Evangelists in particular were anathema to the Communists; Roman Catholics were often shot on sight.

So Eric was given a Red Cross armband to wear at all times and was dubbed 'hospital accountant' to give him an identifiable link to the medical services. Still, when cycling from village to village, the dangers were acute. 'There were constant tortures and killings, burying alive and executions, because no side ever held prisoners,' said Dr McCall.

When visiting the sick or needy in the villages, he and Eric travelled unarmed. When a friend offered McCall a pistol to carry as protection, Eric immediately shouted, 'Don't touch it.' He believed that without weapons you relaxed and depended entirely on God for your safety. It was an attitude, said McCall, that disconcerted and in a sense disarmed the soldiers who confronted them, because they had never met this reaction to aggression before.

In the villages, many of the older folk remembered Eric from his early years in Siaochang with his parents. His father's winning personality had left its mark and ensured Eric a welcome in many a village. He went round at first with an interpreter called Wang Feng Chou, and their day would start with a wobbly bicycle ride. Eric described it once in a vivid dispatch:

It was a perfect day with not a cloud in the sky and a slight north wind blowing us along. Wang is not a good rider, so we went along slowly. He knew all the short cuts, and it's very much easier when you needn't worry about the road. We stopped at a small place, just near Chuan Tyu. It was a carpenter's shop, but also an inn. We only waited about ten minutes, and during that time told the old man what we were doing. The shop was busy: they were preparing many poorer coffins than usual. The old man – about eighty – had the fine courtesy of old China. We left him and passed by the edge of a temple with a large straight tamarisk tree – quite a landmark. In the distance we could see the Japanese flag waving over the town of Chuan Tyu. Periodically their forces, which are very small, go out on their expeditions, but that day we met no one.

The people in the village were busy spinning thread, and as the making of native cloth this year brings in so much the people are all busy at it. The crops in Nan Kung have been largely a failure, only three or four tenths of the usual, and so the making of cloth is helping people to find a living.

As the sun was setting we reached Wang Feng Chou's village and he found me a place to stay. I stayed in the home of the father of one of the Siaochang School boys. It was a very large family of some twenty odd. Last year cholera carried away four of the family within a very short time.

The boy in Siaochang is in his last year at school. His wife turned out of her room to let me have it. They looked after me very well indeed and were kindness itself. They met each night in my room, and the people from round about gathered with us. We started with hymns which I slowly taught them and by the end of the week they had learned several new ones. The old women are the problem, they learn so slowly compared with the others. Each day, I went out to nearby places and had meetings in the mornings and the afternoons, leaving about 4p.m. so as to be back before the sun set.

The whole of this area is riddled with the Eighth Route Army troops. Schools are opened and all below forty-five are forced to go to them. As you come to these villages, the person on guard often has a slate with two or three characters on it, and the people must recognise them before they can pass.

The villages were different in some ways and yet so much the same. One place we got to and asked the way, but no one would say a word to us. We found a cavalry corps was stationed there and everyone was afraid to give any directions. In most places, the people were burdened by the struggle to live, with heavy taxes added on.

The crop had failed, but they were making a little by spinning cotton and weaving cloth. The food is of the poorest. I would stop to gather the people round. First I would speak of their sorrows and burdens; then I would change; I began to show a world that was burdened – the burden of war; the sorrows, the struggles, the Christian struggle for freedom, and before long they began to forget themselves, and think of the burdens of others the whole world over.

It is wonderful to feel oneself one with the people. I remember, one night, being in a very poor home for supper. The small light was so poor that its rays only lit up the nearby things, and the further parts were just dim objects. There was the faint outline of a spinning loom. All day long they work at it right into the dark hours of the night; click, click, click, it goes all the while. I sat with a bowl of 'chiao tyus'. The man of the house was with me. In the dim light the wife could be seen every now and then attending to the fire and preparing the food. The girl used to come to the evening meetings and I can see those great longing eyes, looking up into my face, so eager, so expectant, just like the child in 'The Light of the World'.

As the meal drew to a close, two young men from next door appeared, with their bowl of gruel. They squatted on the floor and started chatting about English customs and ways of eating. They would laugh and then they asked me to speak in English. Soon we would be on to singing. I'd sing in English and then the same piece in Chinese. I'd teach them in Chinese, and while they sang in Chinese, I'd sing in English and we'd all laugh. And so, for the time being, we forget the sorrows of the present in the laughter of fellowship.

Eric's great secret was that he loved people, and could talk to anyone. The Chinese adored him. They soon found him as useful as a buffer in their quarrels as the mission staff had done in Tientsin. 'Li Mu Shi will settle it,' they would say. ('Li' stands for Liddell and 'Mu Shi' means pastor.) 'Ask Li Mu Shi what he thinks about it.'

Li Mu Shi was also good at sweet-talking the Japanese, whose skirmishes with the Eighth Route Army were signalled daily by the repeated crack of gunfire and the clatter of machine guns. 'He would reply to savage or shouted queries with a beaming smile and perfect good nature,' said a colleague:

The Japanese were then indulging in a campaign of petty persecution to try and get rid of the Siaochang missionaries, but against that smiling

calm their efforts broke time and again. Liddell was asked to go to military
HQ to answer questions, and he cycled off alone to the town, seven miles
away. The gendarmerie tried threats, warnings and accusations in vain; Eric
remained cheerful but quite firm.

In order to rejoin his family in Tientsin he had to pass from Chinese-
controlled into Japanese-held territory. Sentries would search his clothes,
and even his shoes, looking for secret letters. On one occasion a Japanese
sentry stopped him and tried to take his compass from him. 'I told them
it was of more value to me than to them,' he explained afterwards. He
was allowed to keep it.

In fact, Eric was not always an innocent traveller. As Florence
recounted later, on his journeys back to Siaochang from seeing the
family in Tientsin, he used to carry contraband money. The Japanese
had abolished Chinese money and brought in their own paper currency
which everyone was obliged to use. If you were caught with the old
money, you could be shot. But the Japanese were not in control of the
country areas, and at Sioachang the hospital, school and pastoral staff
were all paid in the old currency. So this money had to be smuggled in
from the city through the Japanese lines.

Flo and Eric spent ages working out the best place to hide it each
time. On one occasion they had the brainwave of hollowing out a long
French loaf which they stuffed with money and then left the cone
sticking out his haversack. As always, it was an extremely dangerous
ploy. Somehow or other, when he was stopped by the Japanese, he had
to avoid being searched.

Sure enough, after the first leg of his trip, a four-hour train journey,
Eric was stopped by Japanese guards at the station. They asked to see his
passport. Eric at once whipped out his wallet containing photographs of
his two small daughters. He knew how fond the Japanese were of children,
and the guards immediately responded by taking out photos of their own
faraway loved ones to show him. Eric told Flo that he felt very sorry for
them because in no time they were crying. Perhaps the guards sensed
the genuine compassion in this passing traveller which, like the relaxed
air Liddell showed elsewhere in the face of frightening aggression, was
unexpected and disarming. In any event, they slapped him on the back and
sent him on his way without a search. Eric strode off, his loaded French
loaf still poking innocently out of the bag slung over his shoulder.

At the mission hospital, the problems faced by staff went considerably
further than whether their LMS salary would make it safely through

enemy lines. Detailing these in a 1984 BBC documentary, Dr Kenneth
McCall gave a long and wearying list:

> We had the demands of the Japanese in our hospital, the demands of
> Communists taking out patients, executing and burying them. We had
> mass graves. We'd get 250 in one evening who'd all be wounded, the left-
> overs of a village that the Japanese had burned down. They'd have shot
> all the males, taken every animal, eaten all they could and raped all the
> women. And we'd get all that was thrown away.

A doctor at the mission hospital wrote that the peacefulness emanating
from the hospital even under greatest stress came from something Eric
Liddell had taught them:

> We have been able to help the wounded of four armies, the Japanese,
> the Chinese Central Army, the Eighth Route Army and the Chinese
> Army that is helping itself under the Japanese. The local people are not
> unanimous as to which of the first three types of armies they prefer, as
> most people think of their own money and food before their country…
> We have had many visits from troops as they have passed through or used
> our mission as a base for operations… With these visits we usually have a
> huge rush of refugees from the village. We take all the women and children
> into the church. It shows that in their mind we stand for a safe refuge,
> unbroken by the worldly warring outside.

Eric had taught the hospital staff to treat all these soldiers as children of
God. To Eric, said the doctor, there was neither Japanese nor Chinese,
soldier nor civilian: they were all men Christ died for.

The disruptions of war were everywhere. Not even a church service
could escape the shells. Eric described how he was once preparing to
conduct a baptismal service in an outlying area:

> The day before for several hours we heard the distant rumble of guns.
> Sunday dawned, and as we were having breakfast a scouting aeroplane
> circled above us. Round and round it went, then off, only to come back
> again. Rumours of an approaching attack were in the air. Our numbers
> at service were considerably less than we had anticipated, and the people
> from other villages were absent.
>
> I was in the middle of the address to those receiving baptism when
> the attack started. The shells exploded with a terrific noise; afterwards we

found that two had landed fairly near, one being just round the corner from us. There was a silence for a moment and then we continued… No one left the building after the service was over, so we just continued with hymns and witness.

There being no troops here, the Japanese soon entered. There were thirty-one truck-loads of them. They searched every place; they entered the church, but on seeing what it was, left at once, only to pop back a minute later to tell us to get the writing on the outside of the church rubbed off. Their visit was a short one, perhaps four hours in all. Only one person was hurt by an exploding shell. They put up notices in the main street and told the people not to be afraid as they were only out to fight the 'bandits', meaning the Eighth Route Army. They were true to their word; they harmed no one, looted comparatively little, and went.

The suffering Eric saw in those times affected him deeply. Annie Buchan remembered the time he visited a village the Japanese had just left. They had taken one man out of his house for questioning, and when he refused to answer, shot him without more ado. Eric told her afterwards, 'I had nothing to say. I just stood there and then I said, "What could God have done?"' Miss Buchan, a diminutive, white-haired lady in her eighties when she recounted this story at her home in Peterhead in Scotland, was in tears at the memory. 'He had such sympathy,' she said. 'Never a lot of talk, but you could see it on his face. Always on his face.'

Annie Buchan described a constant stream of appallingly injured casualties:

> There was one especially awful one at Huo Cho. Eric found a man just outside the village. The Japs thought they had beheaded him – he was a stout man of forty – but they hadn't. He had a very deep wide slash round his neck. He had been lying five days like that before they found him.
>
> Eric was there and I remember his face. On these occasions you just had nothing to say, but the emotion was there on his face. Mr McCall and Dr Graham took the man in and made a very good job of it. He did live. That man became a Christian, and they found he was an artist.

The man's artwork still hangs in houses all over Edinburgh, because he painted a number of pictures to express his gratitude and Eric sent copies home as presents. (The once star-struck Elsa McKechnie received one for her wedding in 1939.) This is how Eric himself told the story in a letter home:

When journeying back from Tientsin to Siaochang my colleagues and I heard of a wounded man, lying in a temple, twenty miles from our Mission Hospital. No carter would take the risk of taking wounded men, for fear of meeting the Japanese troops on the way. However, one Chinese carter said he would go, if I accompanied him. They have a wonderful confidence in us!!! It would be quite dangerous for him, but I think there was no danger so far as I was concerned.

On Saturday, February 18, the carter started on the journey and some hours later I cycled after him. By evening the carter reached Huo Chu, eighteen miles from Siaochang, where we had our Mission premises. I cycled on to Pei Lin Tyu, three miles further on, to see the Headman of the village and make arrangements for the wounded man to be removed. He lay in the temple about 100 yards outside the village. The temple is a filthy place open to the wind and dust. No one ever comes along to clean it.

No home was open to the wounded man, for if the Japanese descended on them and found that a home had anything to do with the military, it would be destroyed at once, and the lives of those in it would be in danger.

For five days the man had lain in the temple. A friend came there daily to feed him. He lay on a thin mattress on the ground. When we remember that the nights and days are cold and that every night the temperature would be at freezing point, if not well below it, we marvel that he was still alive. The Japanese (a tank and ten motor lorries) were at the next village a mile away.

I told the wounded man we would be back early the next day, and then I returned to Huo Chu. That night, as I lay down, wrapped in my old sheepskin coat, my thoughts turned to the next day. Suppose I met the Japanese, what would I say? I felt for my Chinese New Testament, a book I constantly carried about with me. It fell open at Luke 16. I read until I came to verse 10, and this seemed to me to bring me my answer. 'He that is faithful in that which is least is faithful also in much; and he that is unjust in the least is unjust also in much.' It was as if God had said to me, 'Be honest and straight.' I turned and went to sleep. We started early the next morning. As we approached the first village, there was a man standing in the entrance to it, beckoning us in. We entered the village and as we passed through it the Japanese mechanised troops went round it. We fortunately missed each other.

Many of the roads had been dug up, and were like enlarged trenches, and in clambering out our cart overturned. We reached Pei Lin Tyu early in the day and went to the temple. It was Chinese New Year's Day. People were in the temple burning incense. They were even burning it at the side of the wounded man. I asked the people to come out. I gave them a talk on fresh air being of more value to sick or wounded than air laden with incense smoke. Then I turned to those great words from Micah – 'Wherewith shall I come before the Lord? Shall I come before Him with burnt offerings?... He hath shewed thee, O man, what is good; and what doth the Lord require of thee, but to do justly, and to love mercy, and to walk humbly with thy God?'

We laid the man in the cart and left. On reaching Huo Chu, we heard of another man whom we could pick up by going out of our way a short distance. We decided to go and see. When we reached Pang Chuang we went to see the headman. He and some others led us to one of the out-houses. Several men went in first to warn the wounded man that a foreigner was coming in to see him, but that he need not be afraid. On entering I could see, in the dim light, a man reclining on a bed, dirty rags wrapped about his neck. He was one of six men who had been surrounded by the Japanese. They were told to kneel for execution. Five knelt but the sixth remained standing. When the officer came to him he drew his sword and slashed at him, making a gash from the back of his neck to his mouth. He fell as dead. After the Japanese left the villagers came out, and finding him still alive, they had taken him to this out-house where he had lain for several days.

Eric described the bumpy journey to Siaochang Hospital, eighteen miles away, with Japanese planes circling overhead and troops moving parallel to them a mile away. On reaching the hospital, the first man, the one they had found in the temple, died.

No wonder the Eric Liddell story kept ministers in sermon material for months. Who needed the ancient parable of the Good Samaritan when they had the example of Liddell rescuing a dying man in a temple with relentless incense-burners walking past on the other side of the shrine? The parallels were irresistible, right down to the wandering evangelist doing good among the poor, telling stories to simple people, preaching about the Kingdom of Heaven.

But that really was Eric Liddell as Annie Buchan remembers him:

Oh, he was attractive. His eyes were always shining and he always had a marvellous smile. But he never spoke a lot. He was very quiet. But when he did, he always had something to say. There was just never any doubt

Eric Liddell and Annie Buchan in northern China.

that he had this inner power. All the people loved him. It was his kindness and his attitude towards them. He sympathised with them and assured them how much he cared.

'Eric, how do you really feel?' I asked him once. 'Have you any regrets about leaving a city and a college with high-grade students and coming here, trudging round this district in all weathers?' (because the preaching was always done in the open air, you know). Without any hesitation he said, 'Never. I have never had so much joy and freedom in my work as here.'

But even Tientsin, where Florence and the children carried on with their lives between brief visits from Eric, was hardly a haven of security. The Japanese had firm control there. There was sporadic guerrilla fighting, and tension in the city was mounting daily. Chinese newspapers had been suppressed and Japanese-controlled papers, printed in Chinese, were thrust into every house with a demand for payment. The British newspaper in Tientsin, which was the main source of information for foreigners in North China, ventured a criticism of the Japanese military and was summarily banned, except in the British and French concessions. The Japanese were in control of transport, railways, mail and currency.

The Japanese were also flooding the area with heroin to help finance the war effort. Before the war Eric had watched the heroin-runners in operation between Manchuria and North China. The ticket-collectors on the trains had allowed the pedlars to operate, even in those days of strict Chinese customs control. But now that the Japanese were in charge, drugs were being allowed to pour into China. The cities were also being flooded with cheap Japanese goods.

Eric was glad to take his family out of it all in the summer of 1939 when he went on his second furlough. He travelled with Florence and the girls to Canada first and left them in Toronto with her mother while he returned to Scotland. There he was quickly subsumed in another round of speaking engagements. Scottish friends noticed that he had grown more serious and had lost even more hair. Britain was now at war, and Eric promptly volunteered to be a pilot in the RAF.

Florence often smiled at the thought. Eric, she said, was such a romantic. It was just like him to go for something madly dashing, like being a fighter pilot. And dangerous. It had to be the riskiest job going.

But they turned him down flat: at thirty-seven he was too old for flying duties. But they offered him a desk job, and you might have thought that after all he had been through in China some gentle office work, with a smart uniform and regular leaves with his family, might have held some appeal. But he replied at once, 'If you're only going to stick me behind a desk, then I've got more important work to do.'

Florence and the two girls joined him in Edinburgh in March 1940. Since they were a little squashed all together in Mary Liddell's flat, Eric's sister Jenny offered them the use of her family bungalow at Carcant in the countryside some twenty miles outside the city. They also lent Eric a Baby Austin car to, as Jenny put it, 'tootle around the country in' to their hearts content. Despite the country's war-footing, it was an idyllic few months, with long, lazy days spent swimming and picnicking together, enjoying the novelty of each other's uninterrupted company at last. But by August it was time to leave for Toronto and thence China again. They left carrying the love and fond wishes of their Scottish family – as well as the chickenpox virus which, as they discovered *en route*, Jenny's three-year-old daughter had passed on to her two young cousins before they left.

It proved to be a perilous journey. They boarded at Liverpool on 12 August and joined a fifty-ship convoy, which was being escorted by warships of the Royal Navy for protection. But off the Irish Sea their ship was hit by a torpedo. Eric later described that perilous voyage:

It was 8.30p.m. when the children were asleep. Whether it was a 'dud', and only the cap exploded, or whether it had expended its energy, having been fired from too great a distance, or had exploded right below us, we are not sure. I would say that we were actually hit, and that only the cap exploded, judging from the feel in our cabin. No alarm was given for us to go to the boats, but the signal for all boats to zigzag was given by ours.

The next night we lost one of our ships at the back of the convoy. The sea was choppy – a very difficult one to spot submarines in. The escort left us the next day. This was the hardest of all days. About 10a.m. a small boat about a quarter of a mile from us was torpedoed, blew up, and sank in two minutes; they must have hit the engine boiler. We were on deck ready for the boats, and everyone zigzagged. About noon the 'all-clear' went and we turned to dinner. We had just started, and were half-way through the first course, when the alarm went again. Another boat torpedoed. It didn't sink. We heard later that it was able to get along. Whether it turned back or tried to carry on, I don't know.

We were still in convoy, but not escorted now. By teatime they decided it was too dangerous going on in convoy, so we broke it and each put on full steam ahead… It was a tense time right up to the next morning. At 6p.m. word came through by wireless that the ships which had been sailing next to us, about 200 yards off, for the last two days had been torpedoed. Ten minutes later, another; and at nine o'clock at night we heard that a submarine had risen to the surface and was being engaged by one of the convoy in a running fight.

The ship was running at full speed, far above its average. All night people slept in their clothes, with life-belts ready. The next day the tension eased; we were going out of range of the ordinary submarines; only an ocean-going one could come so far, and there were few of these. The greater speed in the heavy sea caused numbers to be sea-sick again. Since then it has been calmer. No excitement; we have had enough for one trip…

Both the kids are well, except that 'Tricia has developed a cough these last two days. They weren't scared at all, for they didn't really know what it all meant. People on board have been very friendly and the crew have been exceptionally helpful. The loss of life in the sinkings would be small. Of the five ships that went down only two were British. They were all cargo boats. It is estimated that if all perished the total wouldn't be more than eighty. Still, eighty means a lot of sadness and suffering!

They made it at last to Nova Scotia, enjoyed a brief rest in Toronto and were back in Tientsin before the end of October 1940. Eric settled his family in the city and returned to the work at Siaochang. The situation there was now much worse. Siaochang had become a garrisoned village with a high wall. It looked to Eric, staring out from his bedroom window, like 'one of the outposts of the Empire'. He watched a stream of dejected men going out on forced labour to prepare a motor road to pass to the east of Siaochang. He wrote:

> Ruthlessly land is requisitioned without any compensation. Ancient burial places and graves are disregarded as the Japs gradually force their way further in and drive their roots deeper. It is the people who suffer all along. It makes you think of the old Roman press gangs, and brings with it an ever increasing hatred and rebellious spirit that these things should be.

The Japanese had not had an easy time occupying the district. The Chinese Eighth Route Army was not allowing them to settle. Before and during Eric's furlough, battles were raging round the mission compound. Annie Buchan recalled how one day a Japanese officer called to say that they were going to park their carts and ammunition against the hospital, with twenty soldiers on guard over them. They knew that the Chinese would not fire on the hospital. As the morning wore on the noise of battle came closer, and a Japanese officer estimated that by three o'clock the Eighth Route Army would be routed. But two hours later it was the Japanese who were in full retreat, fleeing for their lives.

It was a nerve-racking time. The next day a village near the mission was completely wiped out. Other villages were devastated. Many people died, many more were seriously wounded and once more the casualties poured into the hospital. To make room for them, refugees had to be turned out of the church and housed in the school. The missionaries boiled surgical instruments and changed dressings under the supervision of the hospital staff. And in the middle of it all the Japanese arrived and carried out an inspection of the hospital, while the Chinese schoolchildren lined up and bowed a welcome.

Alex Baxter, a young evangelist who was helping in the hospital that day, was disgusted by the refusal of local Chinese leaders to give the missionaries any help:

> We begged for food for our refugees, but they would give neither grain nor a stove to boil grain. Nothing showed more clearly the fundamental, even startling difference between the Christian outlook and the non-Christian. One would have expected them to share something of the

heavy burden of the Mission. They had seen us caring for hundreds of their own people. We had cared for hundreds and the mind cannot face the thought of what has happened to the many hundreds more who could not come to us.

As Liddell continued his pastoral work around the villages, the tension and fear in the air bit him at every turn in the road. When he approached a village he would invariably spot a man lounging on the outskirts, posted there to warn the village of approaching danger. When he went to a church to conduct a wedding, people were too afraid to come out and join him for worship on the eve of the ceremony. He described the wedding:

Saturday was the great day. The bridegroom goes his rounds first thing, paying his respects to all who are related to him or are taking part in the ceremony. At ten o'clock the people had gathered in the church. The bridegroom was there with all the splendour of new clothes, a red sash round his waist and over his shoulder, and a great paper flower on his chest. The bride arrived in a chair and came out at the entrance to the church. It was a cold, windy day, and she looked cold. Although the place was filled, and there were many children present, they were all as quiet as could be during the whole service.

After the bowing was over and the benediction pronounced we turned and went to where the bridal dinner was prepared. And so, in the midst of all the fears and alarms, the world goes on as if all were calm and quiet. The heavier guns could be heard that evening only a mile away, as they fired in the direction of the people who were cutting up the road. But in Huo Chu we just met together for a service of prayer, praise and thanks, thinking about our contribution to a better world; and the bridal pair spent their first night with the sound of gunfire in their ears, but love and joy in their hearts.

I stayed on over Sunday, taking the service and chatting with the people. I should have returned that day, but the cart I was expecting did not arrive till nightfall. It had been delayed by the Eighth Army, who were stopping the moving of all carts. On our return journey today there was little of incident except at one point. The enemy must have taken us for the Eighth Army and fired two shots. We just got off our bikes and stayed still till they realised their mistake, and then we went on.

My work will be going round the various churches. I now go out to the south-west to a part I have never visited before. When I am out it is giving, giving, all the time, and trying to get to know the people, and trying to leave them a message of encouragement and peace in a time when there is no external peace at all.

By now the missionaries were beginning to realise that their time in Siaochang could be coming to an end. It was obvious that sooner or later the British in China, hitherto at least tolerated by the Japanese, would be regarded as the enemy, and then their days of freedom would be numbered. The country was in chaos. The war that had started with a patched-up unity between the Nationalists and the Communists and was fought on a united Chinese front against the Japanese, had become a war of two Chinas. The Red Army and the Nationalist army were attacking the invader separately, and at the beginning of 1941 Chiang Kai-shek's government and the Communists stopped talking to each other altogether. Supplies were cut off from Communist armies all over the country. A blockade of government troops was thrown about the Communist civilian base in northern Shensi and it was sealed off. So now the government troops were fighting the Japanese, the Communists were fighting the Japanese and the government troops were fighting the Communists.

In this senseless game, the invading Japanese had a field day and swarmed across the country. But they did not have it all their own way. A correspondent writing in 1942 was impressed by the unflinching determination of the exceedingly young Chinese soldiers. Describing what it was like after the Chinese victory over the Japanese in the ten-day battle of Changsha, in central Hunan, he wrote:

And now from everywhere there appeared blue-helmeted soldiers in light blue padded cotton uniforms. They were all young. They walked in the sunlight out of the shelter of bomb holes with an unexpected swagger, their bayonets gleaming. We photographed them. They smiled. They were very eager to talk about the battle, and they mentioned Colonel Li, who had defended the city from within, with extraordinary respect and affection. 'A general or an officer who obtains the respect of his soldiers in China can work miracles,' someone said, and it was easy to believe him, for these youths, fingering their bayonets and gazing dreamily at the passing coffins, are soldiers of whom any country could be proud. They were nearly all Hunanese, fighting for their homes – farmers' lads, mostly, with faces like ripe apples and a gay swing in their movements. All winter they had been waiting. To while the time away, they had planted vegetables on their blockhouses, and it was curious to turn into a side street and see, through a curtain of bayonets, lettuces sprouting above corrugated-iron houses.

We followed the soldiers along a broken street, where the charred buildings were still smoking. Occasionally only a single wooden post would remain standing. A tree stump or a lamp-post with bullet holes was like a wound still bleeding, but those bullet marks on wooden posts were so fresh that they seemed to have been made only a few moments before. Here the nakedness of war appeared in all its violence, for bodies still lay in the houses, and the sound of pickaxes echoed in the still wintry morning. It was strangely quiet... High above the city aeroplanes flew and fought in the cold winter sun... When they had gone, the city was more silent than ever, until suddenly we heard the sound of squealing pigs and turning a corner we watched three Hunanese peasants wheeling their barrows, with immense centre wheels and curved flanks, which were so delicately carved that they would grace a museum of modern industrial art. The barrows contained children in bright red leggings and woollen mufflers, and their expressions were oddly at variance with the expressions of the peasants, who looked grimed and sad with too much wandering. Behind the peasants came the squealing pigs. The peasants told us that they were going back to their homes on the west bank of the river, and their faces under their black turbans lit with relief when the soldiers gave them a right of way.

The Japanese had attempted to gain possession of the burial mound which overlooked the city. From there, with their heavy guns, they could dominate the fortress. And everything in their plans they achieved except that they failed to bring up any heavy guns at all, for the roads were cut by the partisans. They had obeyed the pure theory, and failed to make it a reality. They fought a battle of the imagination, and inevitably they failed.

The year before that battle, Eric and his colleagues bad been forced to evacuate the mission compound at Siaochang. They had known for weeks it was coming, for they sensed the attitude of the Japanese changing. At the beginning of the war, the invaders had treated the British with a measure of civility; they might have wandered through the hospital sticking their swords into the dressings, but the redoubtable Annie Buchan was in charge and she knew how to put them in their place. Now the soldiers started coming into their homes drunk and brandishing their swords. One day Annie rushed into the hospital operating theatre, looking urgently for a doctor, and found that a soldier had pinned the doctor against the wall and was hitting him with his baton. She marched up, grabbed the doctor and said, 'I want this doctor.' The soldier fell back in sheer astonishment. It was clear to her that there had been a shift in authority: the officers no longer made any effort to control their men.

Early in 1941, the missionaries were told to pack their bags and leave. They had two weeks to get ready, but were then told they could take nothing with them. They handed over the keys of their house to the Japanese and set off along the road to the railway station on their last journey to Tientsin. They heard later that Siaochang had been destroyed, every last brick and plank of it.

Amid the turmoil in the countryside Eric had been growing increasingly worried about the safety of his family in Tientsin. Was it right to keep them there when foreigners were liable to be interned at any time? Patricia and Heather were aged only five and four and Florence was expecting another baby. The decision, taken with the board of the missionary society, was that they should leave for the safety of Canada. Florence recalls:

> It was a very difficult decision. I didn't want to come away at all, but we were sure Japan was going to come into the Second World War. Eric could have come with us, but he didn't feel he should. He said he would feel so much better if I had the children in Canada. He was worried that if they took us hostage, he didn't think he could trust himself. No, I never felt his work came first. It wasn't like that at all. He just felt others were staying and he ought to as well.

Eric thought the safest way of crossing the Pacific would be on a Japanese ship, so they booked a passage on the *Nita Maru* and in May 1941 travelled to the port of Kobe in Japan to say goodbye. Eric accompanied them to their cabin. Before leaving, he lifted Patricia on to his knee and said he wanted her to help Mummy, to help take care of Heather and to help with the new baby when it came. She hugged him and promised she would. When the loudspeaker announced that the ship was about to set sail, he scooped the girls into his arms for a final cuddle. Then he hugged and kissed his beloved Flo, and rushed away. She burst into tears.

Did the thought flit through Eric's mind as he strode away from them across the pier that day, resplendent as ever in his white shorts and knee-length socks, that he might never see his family again? For all that her heart ached as she waved one last time from the rail of the *Nita Maru*, it certainly never occurred to Florence: 'It just never crossed my mind for a minute. I thought it would be one or two years. Even right at the end it never crossed my mind that anything could happen to Eric. I don't know how I could have been so naïve.'

9

'Days of Perplexity
Like the Present'

In September 1941 Eric received a telegram from Toronto telling him of the birth of his third daughter, Maureen, the child he was never to see.

By this time he was living in Tientsin again, sharing a flat in the French concession with A.P. Cullen, who had been one of his schoolmasters at Eltham College and latterly a senior colleague on the staff of the Tientsin Anglo-Chinese College. (He was later to write the biography of Lavington Hart of Tientsin, and an edifying book called *Making China's Men*).

For the first time in his life, Eric had no definite job to engage his energies, but he kept busy. He worked on a *Manual of Christian Discipleship*, which he hoped would be translated into Chinese for the guidance of Chinese pastors. It included sixty pages of Bible readings, with comments for every day of the year. He spent long hours working on that project, but never deviated from the practice that had become his routine, of rising early and hallowing the 'silent hour' which shaped the rest of his day.

There is something about Eric Liddell's silent hour, something about his self-discipline and his ideal of the mind, body and spirit working together in obedience to God, which is strongly reminiscent of the Oxford Group, that remarkable evangelistic movement that seized the hearts of so many young students in the 1920s and 1930s. The basic theology of the Oxford Group, in simplified form, was that an individual should confess his sins, accept Jesus Christ as his personal saviour and share his experience with others whose lives had been changed in this way. It emphasised, indeed demanded, four cardinal principles of honesty, purity, unselfishness and love, reinforced by compulsory public 'sharings'. Frank Buchman, the American evangelist who founded the Group movement and was later to become associated with the much more politically orientated 'Moral Rearmament', had been on an evangelistic mission to China in 1918, where he had held the first of the group's famous house parties. All kinds of people were in close session for two weeks: missionaries, pastors, statesmen, businessmen and professional people. It could be that Eric Liddell's missionary father also attended, in which case he may have conveyed something of the excitement of the new movement to his teenage son.

Eric came into contact with members of the group himself over the years and derived much spiritual nourishment from these times. In 1924, in the summer after the Olympics, he met a young man by the name of Loudon Hamilton at an athletics meeting in Galashiels in Scotland. Hamilton had met Buchman while studying at Oxford and through him had rediscovered the personal faith which had died with his comrades in the mud of Passchendaele and the Somme. Eric was impressed by Hamilton's description of the great adventure of discovering God's guidance by listening to Him every morning during a quiet time and the implications for his own life. His year of evangelism with D.P. Thomson before he left for China was much influenced by these insights.

During his furlough in Scotland in February 1932, a member of the Oxford Group spoke at an informal meeting at his parents' home in Edinburgh. Physically and emotionally exhausted by the demands of his college course and his heavy schedule of speaking engagements, Eric listened keenly as the speaker talked of the need for complete surrender to God each day. He felt re-energised. At a meeting of group members in Edinburgh later that year, he told them that he wanted to associate himself with the Oxford Group because its members had challenged him to a keener faith and practice. He would return to China, he said, leading a fuller Christian life than when he first went out.

It is clear that Liddell incorporated many of the Oxford Group principles into his daily routine and believed that these helped him to lead a Christ-centred life. When people described him as 'Christ-like', they were seeing in Eric Liddell something which was not merely a matter of charmed personality or effortlessly dynamic faith, but rather the product of day-by-day discipline and personal commitment to prayer and to the embodying of prayer in action.

However, the practices of the movement were not to everyone's taste. Annie Buchan, the small and feisty Siaochang matron, was suspicious of what she felt was a trend towards exclusiveness in the Oxford Group. When Eric's brother Rob Liddell and another missionary, William Rowlands (author of *The Plain and the People*), came back to Siaochang from furlough with their wives and started holding confessional group sessions at the mission, she didn't like it:

I had read Buchman's book and I liked it very much, but when two missionary families come back to a small community and set up a special group, to me it's a bit fishy. I went to their meetings and I found the confessionals not to my liking. I said to Will Rowlands one day, 'If we're going to have meetings the Chinese can't come to, we're making a division.' I said I wouldn't come to the confessionals again. And because I wouldn't go, the rest of the hospital staff wouldn't go either.

This difference of opinion happened long before Eric was posted to Siaochang. Annie Buchan said:

Eric wasn't in it, and we never discussed it. I think by then everyone had realised that we couldn't afford a split. The 'Inner Circle' disappeared. Eric was not, to my knowledge, ever a member of the inner circle; it was mostly over before he came. But some of it would have suited him; their principles were very good. From my point of view, the problem was the confessionals; to me it was a break in our fellowship.

It is unlikely that the tendency towards spiritual elitism (at least as interpreted by Annie Buchan) would have had much appeal for Eric Liddell. It is hard to imagine him being attracted to any clique that excluded his flock, the Chinese. Rather it was the principles which invigorated him. His friend Howard Smith, a Methodist missionary in the English concession in Tientsin, wrote of the effect of the Oxford Group on him:

Upon his life this movement had only a good effect, for it deepened and strengthened what was already there... Eric was applying to all he did and said the 'Four Standards'; but he did not do it openly or blatantly. You just knew that those standards were there, always, as an undertone to all he did.

These months in Tientsin after his family left must have been a frustrating period for Eric, when he felt he had nothing positive or constructive to do. But in December 1941 everything changed drastically, for him and millions of others across the world, when the Japanese launched their airborne assault on Pearl Harbour in the Pacific. Within weeks, the members of the London Missionary Society were ordered to leave their homes within the French concession. Eric Liddell and six other missionaries were taken into the hospitable homes of members of the English Methodist Mission in the British concession. Eric and three of

Eric Liddell.

his colleagues crammed in with Howard Smith's family in the Methodist Mission compound, where they would stay for over a year. They were free to move about the streets, wearing armbands to display their nationality, but were not allowed outside the concession.

Many of Eric's colleagues really felt at a loose end, but Eric managed to keep himself busy. The Japanese would not permit any assemblies of more than ten people, which effectively put an end to church services. But Eric thought up the idea of a rota of reverends who would prepare a sermon in turn for each Sunday; the wives would then invite guests to tea on Sunday afternoons, making sure that each individual company never numbered more than ten. Sufficient copies of the sermon would be run off to ensure that each tea-party was able to have a short service round the tea-table, and the sermons were handed round with the tea-cakes.

This period of comparative inaction must have been a strain for a man whose constant urge was to be up and doing. He played cricket with the sons of the Methodist staff; he taught tennis to their daughters in the blazing heat; he made up fours for bridge. He once queued for bread at 5a.m. for his host's family, and got up at the crack of dawn another morning to sweep the house from top to bottom after a dust storm. He wrote long letters to Florence and eagerly read her news of the children's progress. How he longed to see his new baby.

D.P.Thomson cites a letter from Eric at this time, showing that he was thinking of applying for repatriation. Everyone was asked to sign a form saying whether or not he wanted to stay. Eric had wanted to remain, but then so many others decided to do the same thing that he felt be could perhaps be spared to do more useful work elsewhere than he was doing in China. He wrote to ask Florence what she thought about him working for a Home Mission in Canada. He felt that the need out there was great, and if he got back he might like to have a crack at it. Soon, however, the decision would be taken out of his hands.

The fate of the missionaries in China was not exactly front-page news in Britain, a country that was being bombed at home and had men fighting across half the world. As the enemy of Japan, China was now an ally and Madame Chiang Kai-shek's fundraising tours were occasionally brought to the notice of the public, who added 'Aid to China' to their list of flag days. But for the most part, missionary magazines and reports were the only publications that relatives could scan for some hint of what was happening to Eric Liddell and the hundreds like him. How gratefully people at home must have seized on these for scraps of information about their loved ones, although the news was frequently grim. Decades later it is still moving to read of the everyday dramas and mounting anxieties of missionary life as the Japanese invasion took a grip across the country. They leap out at you from the columns of *China's Millions*, the magazine of the China Inland Mission, with such force that a few sentences here and there are enough to capture a sense of the strain those missionaries were living under:

• **We must remind our friends** that we are no longer allowed to transmit personal gifts to missionaries in China as in pre-war days.

• **At the present moment no British women** are allowed to sail for 'occupied' China and we have to suspend, just for the moment, the training of women recruits.

• **When the Japanese occupied Changtze**, where Miss Lundgren and Miss Bachmann were stationed, the ladies were cut off from all supplies and lived for four months on a diet of millet porridge three times a day... Miss Bachmann's health – she had been suffering from digestive trouble – greatly improved. It is interesting to hear that an American Mission doctor in Peking has discovered the virtues of millet porridge for digestive trouble and now gives it a regular place on her own menu, and feeds her friends on it, too.

• **After Mr Kenneth Price had escorted his wife to Siaochang** for medical attention and returned to Kienteh, the Japanese attack and capture of Siaochang took place. So Mr Price is now separated from his wife, he still in Free China and she in Japanese-occupied territory.

• **One of the senior Japanese officers in Kaifeng**... has been very friendly during the last few weeks as a result of Dr Hess having located, by means of the hospital X-ray machine, a bullet which had lodged in his chest. He has since brought his wife along for medical treatment.

• **It is encouraging to note that in days of perplexity like the present**, the leaders of our Mission in China are not contemplating retreat, or withdrawal, but are even planning for advance.

• **The last foreign missionary** has been driven out of Turkestan.

• **Deaths**: At Siakiang, Mrs H. Sames, from bombing injury; at Tachu, Szechwan, Esther Grace Simmonds, aged 10½ months, from dysentery; at Chengku, Mr Arnold Strange, of typhus; at Chefoo, Frank Sidney Barling, from typhoid fever.

• **It would be difficult to exaggerate the gravity** of the situation in the Far East... Many of our friends will feel deep concern about the staff and the children in the Chefoo schools.

• **Every bed in the hospital** is filled. There is a waiting list of drug addicts. I took in the fifty-eighth today.

• **The Japanese** erected electrified barricades around the British concession in Tientsin, stationing sentries and police at the various entrances and exits.

• **The Generalissimo** [Chiang Kai-shek], speaking in Chunking to a missionary group, said: 'We still need and welcome Christians from other lands who will serve the people. Do not feel that you are guests. You are comrades working with us to serve and save our people and to build a new nation.'

• **Mme Chiang Kai-shek**, when speaking to members of the American Bible Society, during her visit to USA, stated that she and the Gen had arranged that Chinese scholars make a new translation of the Psalms, which had been completed, and of the New Testament, which was in process of translation.

• **The Chinese ambassador to the United States**, a Buddhist, said recently: 'As an unreconstructed heathen I wish to pay my respects to all the Christian missionary workers who have aided China during these years of her struggle. Many of these missionaries have lost their property, have suffered physical injury. Their women have suffered grave indignities, physical hardships and misery, but so far as I know, no missionary has deserted his post.'

• **From Mr and Mrs Crane, on the Burma Border**: 'The fight was on… We wasted a morning packing for flight. Then, as the next morning greeted us with still more livid flames from a third village burning, we wasted a second hour or so discussing where to flee, and then, as everything had continued quiet, we wasted a third hour unpacking to stay!'

• **The Chefoo Schools**. The entire schools have been interned by the Japanese together with all other foreign residents, in the compound of the American Presbyterian Mission in Chefoo. No further news has since been received… We understand that the Japanese marched into the schools and took possession of a section of the premises on August 27th and pressed for the complete evacuation of the whole building.

• **Famine Conditions**. Our readers will doubtless have seen in the press reference to the appalling famine conditions affecting many millions in a part of the Province of Honan. We understand that thousands have been dying of starvation. It is reported that Madame Chiang has allocated a substantial amount to famine relief from the gift she has received through Lady Cripps' Fund… If any feel constrained to do something for the relief of these stricken people they can send their contribution to… the British Fund for the Relief of Distress in China.

• **Madame Chiang Kai-shek**. It will be known that this noble Christian lady is now in the United States for medical treatment, and prayer should be offered on her behalf for a complete and speedy recovery. It has been rumoured that Madame Chiang will visit this country after her stay in the USA… It was deeply interesting to notice that in allocating funds… Madame Chiang gave a large proportion of the money to Christian enterprises.

• **Sino-British Friendship**. We heartily welcome the cordial and friendly relationship which exists between the rulers and people of China and ourselves... The record of our dealings with China in years gone by has not been what we could have wished, but there is evidently a sincere desire on the part of our rulers to express sympathy with China in her present difficulties and future aspirations. The proposal to abandon all extra-territorial rights in China is an evidence of this, and is a move in the right direction.

• **Missionaries in Occupied China**. News has come to us that all the British and Americans in Shanghai, Tientsin and Tsingtao were being interned... A cablegram informs us that the following missionaries were interned in Yangchow, where one of the camps established by the Japanese is situated. It is probably the Women's Language School of the CIM in which they are interned: Mr and Mrs A.L. Keeble, Millin, Price, Scott, Weller, Fleischmann, Hayman.

• **The Problem of Finance in China**. One of the serious difficulties... is the continuing and uncontrolled soaring of prices of all necessities, and the situation is aggravated by the Chinese having 'pegged' the exchange for sterling at 80 dollars to the £1. A more just exchange would probably be ten times as much... Recent letters state that in Chunking a suit of clothes costs £60 to £70, a pair of socks £5, potatoes 1s 2d a lb. Wages of servants are now so fantastically high to make it virtually impossible to employ any.

• **Through the kind offices of the Minister of Finance** it has been arranged that money sent out for missions and for philanthropic purposes shall receive a bonus of fifty per cent on the exchange... but this is rather nullified by the still higher rise in prices.

• **A missionary doctor**, Catherine Simmons, described the famine in Honan Province: 'Military grain taxes have been getting heavier and heavier, and ever since I have been in Honan strings of carts have been streaming out of the Province, loaded with military wheat. So there were no reserves. Then last year's wheat was a very poor crop. The summer following was the longest, hottest, driest known for over thirty years at least, and most of the autumn crops of sweet potatoes, beans, etc., perished in the drought.

'I was in Western Glory [Sihwa] through the summer, and Joel describes, far better than I could ever hope to, what we saw there when the locusts came. On streamed the unbroken ranks, set in battle array. It was not exactly the garden of Eden before them, but at least there were the remnants of the autumn crop that had survived the drought, and on which so much hope was set, but behind them was a desolate wilderness – the bare, brown land stripped of every vestige of green.

'The city's gods were carried out to bake in the sunshine, and day and night gongs and drums were beaten before them as prayers were made to the powers of evil to possess a man so that he might prophesy when rain would come. . . The urgent need for rain was that next year wheat might be planted; only a month to planting time; only three weeks; only two – and then the dykes of the Yellow River gave way and the waters swept over the plain, right into the outskirts of the city, and the last hope of planting wheat was gone!

'These last months of winter have been the worst, and some could not face them, so had one last, tasty meal, the last mouthful of which was so prepared that next day they wouldn't have to worry about food.'

• **Interned Missionaries**. Not much news is reaching us from our friends who are interned, but from what little information has come out ... the spirit and cheerful courage displayed is deeply moving and impressive… There is still some hope that there be a small repatriation of a small number of internees.

• **From a missionary in West Yunnan**. Arrival of Superintendent from a journey to the Salween River to try to get in touch with the Hattons who were cut off by the Jap advance last year. He was unsuccessful… but we found he had with him a young American pilot who had to bale out of his plane after getting his oil pipe hit by a stray Jap bullet fired from the ground… Hattons arrived here two days ago, safe and well!

• **Report from Yangchow**. We saw first-hand something of the methods used by the invader toward a conquered people – economic pressure to the point where they can hardly exist because of high prices on one hand, and acute shortage of necessities on the other – in short, terrorism and despotism: the most insidious method used to undermine the morale is the introduction of narcotics – opium, heroin, to which thousands are victims.

• **Health Services in China**. It has been computed that each day there are 16 million sick persons in China; the yearly death roll is 10 million, of whom 4 million need not die if adequate medical attention were available. It would probably be true to say that the organisation of present health services in China is largely due to the work of the medical missionary in former years. Whatever might be the estimate in which medical missionary service is held by people at home, the Chinese are more than ever convinced, especially through their experiences during the war years, that missionaries have a genuine love for the people themselves.

- **Stop Press**. We deeply regret to have to record the death of Mrs Hoyte, wife of Dr Stanley Hoyte, at Lanchow on December 19th from typhus. (Mrs Hoyte had left her six children with the Principal of the school at Chefoo to join her husband at Kansu in 1940.)
- **Interned Missionaries**. Messages from the internment camps indicate that living conditions are tolerable… From a repatriated missionary comes news of … the Boys' School recently removed from Chefoo to Weihsien, where there are 2000 Allied nationals interned. The Japanese were said to be acting towards the children with consideration.

These reports give a flavour of the human cost of the missionaries' dedication to their calling in this tortured nation. Many stayed long past the time when any regard for their own safety should have prompted them to leave. When repatriation was offered, many turned it down, until eventually it was too late. In Tientsin, the Japanese were tightening their grip on the Europeans, and Eric Liddell and his colleagues were left wondering what their fate was to be. The name Weihsien, soon to appear in the despatches home so eagerly passed on in the columns of *China's Millions*, was about to become all too familiar.

10

'It's Complete Surrender'

When you hear that Eric Liddell died in a Japanese internment camp on 21 February 1945, you immediately think of brutality and beatings and starvation, a heroic death in the face of dirt and disease and inhuman cruelty. It is the way thousands of ordinary men and women met their end in the Far East in those terrible years. But it wasn't like that for Eric Liddell. And in a sense it makes the story of his death paradoxically all the more moving.

If he had fallen to a Japanese bayonet or a Samurai sword, or if he had stopped one of the bullets he managed to dodge in the no-man's-land around Siaochang, or if he had even died of straight hunger at Weihsien internment camp, it would have fitted much better the romantic image that the public had bestowed on him since the distant glory days at the Paris Olympics. It would have completed the myth-making. Yet the manner of Eric Liddell's dying is poignant precisely because it was not particularly heroic. It was as untheatrical as the man himself.

He died, at the age of forty-three, because something had gone wrong with the chemistry of his body. He fell prey to a fatal disease, but its effects were slow and painful, and although he bore the pain with the same gritty determination he had always displayed on the racetrack, the irony is that the disease came to affect the aspect of him that had always been his strength, the attribute that, permeated by his relationship with God, had enabled him to move men and mountains. That was his personality itself. It wasn't that he changed from a sunny-natured optimist into a disagreeable curmudgeon: he remained kind and considerate to others right to the end. But he fell victim to bouts of depression that were totally alien to the real Eric Liddell, and which made him feel a failure to the faith that had always buttressed him.

But a failure was the last thing he would be called, even at the end. Especially at the end.

On 12 March 1943, Eric Liddell and his colleagues in Tientsin received the call, along with hundreds of other British, American and assorted 'enemy nationals', to go to the Civil Assembly Centre at Weihsien in Shantung Province, just to the south of Peking. Ever since the attack on Pearl Harbour in December 1941 and America's full-scale entry into the Second World War, it had only been a matter of time before the foreigners in Japanese-occupied China would be interned. Fortunately, since no resistance had been offered to the Japanese in Peking or Tientsin, they were to be classified not as prisoners of war but as 'civil internees'.

The British were to go in three parties, and Eric was appointed captain of the missionaries' group in the third party. They were given until 26 March to send their luggage ahead, each allowed three trunks plus bed and bedding. Two suitcases could be carried as hand luggage on the journey, which enabled them to take several personal effects along. But nobody warned them that eating utensils would have been useful, too.

On 30 March they assembled at 7.30p.m. and their luggage was inspected by the Japanese guards. Two hours later they marched off down the streets of Tientsin to the railway station. Allied personnel from all over North China had been rounded up in this way, and in both Peking and Tientsin the spectacle was the same: hundreds of British and Americans of all ages and all backgrounds struggling along the streets with their luggage. Sympathetic Chinese onlookers lined the streets to see them go. It was stage-managed by the Japanese as a spectacle of humiliation.

They were bundled into third-class railway carriages, missionaries and businessmen, society ladies and prostitutes, nurses and secretaries, all together. At 11.40p.m., their train moved out and most of the passengers sat up all night. They changed trains at Tainan next morning, and arrived at Weihsien at 3.40 in the afternoon. The camp was about two miles from the city.

The compound was small, only about 150 by 200 yards: very small for 1,800 people to live in. Ironically, it was a ruined American Presbyterian mission station, grey and institutional like all the foreign mission stations. Its Chinese name meant the Courtyard of the Happy Way. As the internees straggled in, they noticed a school, a hospital and a church. Some might have been observant enough to spot three kitchens and some bakery ovens. What everyone did notice was that the place was wrecked. The buildings themselves were undamaged, but the insides were a shambles. The contents had been thrown on to the streets, which were strewn with old beds and radiators and bits of piping and broken desks and classroom chairs.

The newcomers were led to their quarters. Unattached men and women went to dormitories; married couples and their children found themselves in rooms measuring 13ft by 9ft. That night in countless rows of these small rooms families were trying to sort themselves out, to the inevitable accompaniment of children's tears.

Sooner or later that first evening, the new internees felt called upon to inspect the camp's toilet arrangements. The shock they received has stayed with many of them to this day. Langdon Gilkey, until then a young instructor at Yenching Anglo-American University near Peking, one of the Christian Colleges in China, describes his first impressions in the book he wrote after it was all over, *Shantung Compound: The Story of Men and Women under Pressure*:

> As we entered the door of the Men's Room, the stench of what assailed our Western nostrils almost drove us back into the fresh March air. To our surprise, we found the brand-new fixtures inside: Oriental-style toilets with porcelain bowls sunk into the floor, over which we uncomfortably had to squat. Above them on the wall hung porcelain flushing boxes with long metal pull-chains, but – the pipes from the water tower outside led only into the men's showers; not one was connected with the toilets. Those fancy pipes above us led nowhere. The toilet bowls were already filled to overflowing. With no servants, no plumbers and no running water anywhere in camp, it was hard to see how they would ever be unstopped.

Their depression mounted as they were led to another part of the compound for supper:

> I saw stretching before me for some seventy yards, a line of quiet, grim people standing patiently with bowls and spoons in their hands… Could human patience bear such a long wait three times a day for meals? However, I joined the line, and three quarters of an hour later we reached the table where thin soup was being ladled out with bread. That was supper. Fortunately there were 'seconds' of bread, because we were very hungry after our long train trip without food.
>
> Our meal finished, we lined up again to have our bowls and spoons washed by women from Tsingtao. The patterns of chores in the new situation were beginning to come clear. As I went out past the steam-filled kitchen with its great Chinese cauldrons, I saw three men from our Peking group being shown how to use the cooking equipment by the men from Tsingtao, turned into 'experts' by their three days of practice.

Before many days were out they were all becoming practised. Society ladies who had scarcely seen the inside of a kitchen before had to scrub floors and wash dishes. There was bread to be baked and water to be drawn; the interior of the compound had to be rebuilt, the meals cooked, the walls mended, the fires stoked, the furniture restored. 'Thus,' wrote Gilkey, 'bank clerks, professors, salesmen, missionaries, importers and executives became bakers, stokers, cooks, carpenters, masons, and hospital orderlies.'

Administration went ahead with typical Japanese efficiency. The camp was divided into three groups, according to their origin in Tientsin, Peking or Tsingtao (now Quingdao). Each group ate its meals together in a large dining room at long wooden tables. Each person had to supply his own cup, plate and cutlery.

Nine departments were set up to coordinate camp duties and each department had its own committee. There were also the Christian Fellowship of the Protestant Churches, the Women's Auxiliary and the Homes Committee (to help women in their homes). The Employment Committee called for a minimum of three hours' work each day from every medically fit man and woman in the camp. There was no Chinese labour to do the menial duties; every job had to be done by internees.

They gradually settled into a rhythm. Everybody would get up on the dot of 7a.m. and attend to the chores. It might be drawing water from the well or sweeping up coal dust to make into brickettes for heating. Men who once had owned coalmines had to scrabble on their hands and knees for that coal dust. It was mixed with earth and put into tubes made from the tins of baby milk that the Red Cross brought in from the Swiss Embassy. These were left to dry and then became fuel. Old people and invalids relied on others considerate enough to do their chores.

The internees were not officially prisoners, so there was generally little harassment by the guards. But twice daily roll-calls, whatever the weather and whatever your occupation at the time, tried everyone's nerves. Food was in short supply and people were soon looking thin and wan. They were always hungry.

A Canadian missionary at the camp sent this account to D.P. Thomson:

After the first month, English-language newspapers were delivered once a week. They were printed in Peking or Japan, and carried only German and Japanese news dispatches but gave a fair representation of the war situation in Europe, and one could usually infer what was the course of events in the Pacific. Every major event was heralded as a Japanese victory! But does a victorious army always retreat?

Before going to camp, American and British nationals who had run out of funds were able to obtain a monthly living allowance loan from their home government through the Swiss representative. This was paid in advance to the end of April. In camp, we could receive on application a 'comfort allowance' of about one tenth of the living allowance. In this way we were not without funds. There were regulations, of course. The money was paid to the commandant and released to us at his discretion, but we received some consideration.

For a nondescript population of 1,800 of several nationalities and various religious and irreligious persuasions, whose liberties were curtailed, it is obvious that some clashes with the guards would be likely, but these were rare and there were no serious developments. Fortunately there were no attempts to escape – such an attempt would probably have failed and undoubtedly would have brought punishment to those who remained and a more rigid discipline. There was an intermittent over-the-wall black market where many things were purchased – everything from eggs to opium…

After the first six weeks the authorities opened a canteen where a very limited stock was on sale. There we could occasionally purchase peanuts, peanut oil, eggs, candy, honey, fruit in season, toothpaste, shoe polish, Chinese shoes and clogs, and a variety of other things. The work of the canteen was done by our own people.

As they settled down, the internees began to organise their own entertainment programmes. First these were put on once a week, then twice a week in response to popular demand. There were plays, revues, choral programmes, even symphony concerts. On one occasion the audience was treated to Handel's *Messiah*, another time to a full performance of Mozart's *Concerto in D Minor* (minus double basses and tuba). The culmination of the dramatic enterprises was a full-scale performance of Shaw's *Androcles and the Lion*. It was staged, according to Langdon Gilkey, 'with three complete sets, a full-sized lion made of cloth, cardboard, and armour and helmets for ten Roman guards soldered together out of tin cans from the Red Cross parcels'.

On Sundays there was a variety of church services, with hymn singing in the evening. They even had their own Salvation Army band to play hymns in an open square on Sunday mornings, followed by requests, and an hour's playing outside the hospital. Boy Scouts and Girl Guides continued to meet, and the diligent ones were awarded special Weihsien badges. There were more than a hundred adult education classes on offer in various subjects, including religion, mathematics, painting and philosophy, though there were few takers. The professional teachers banded together to provide a school for the children.

There were hundreds of children in the camp, many without parents. About 300 had come from the Chefoo school run by the China Inland Mission in the port of Chefoo (Yantai) in Shantung, 500 miles north of Shanghai. It was a school for the children of missionaries 'situated on the curve of a quiet bay with a yellow sea-front and a range of hills behind it,' as one described it later. 'In a land of famine, poverty, banditry, civil wars and floods, it was a haven of peace for generations of missionaries' children.' It was run as a British public school, with cricket, football, hockey, rowing and tennis.

Both the town of Chefoo and the school had been captured by the Japanese in 1938. A flurry of lorries, a flash of gun-boats in the harbour, and the job was done. Chefoo school settled again into its old rhythm. In August 1941 most of the children left for home, but many were left behind. As the Japanese pushed inland and anti-British feeling intensified, the school leaders began to discuss the possibility of evacuating before Britain and the USA became directly involved in the Far East war. But the mission leaders were asked not to organise a mass exodus which would panic the Chinese public. Then came Pearl Harbour, and in 1942 the children moved to the American Presbyterian Mission at Temple Hill to the west of the city. Their next move was to Weihsien internment camp, where they arrived in September 1943, six months after Eric Liddell.

Imagine, then, what life was like at Weihsien. It was an over-populated camp where the only privacy anyone had was an area of 9ft by 54ins round the bed; a place peopled by bored children, frustrated teenagers and confused old people, by the widest range of personalities, all rubbing up against each other, queuing for the toilets and the meals and the roll-call and the chores, nerves grinding and personalities clashing, with no escape. All the familiar creature comforts were gone, all the structures by which people organise their lives had been turned upside down.

It is hardly surprising that there were tensions; and one of the most marked of the dissonances was between the businessmen and the missionaries. Langdon Gilkey suggests that there had developed in the Far East 'a chasm of distrust and contempt between merchant and missionary', which was thrown into sharp relief when the two groups found themselves stuck in the same compound for years.

'Most of the Westerners in China detested the missionary, and never were able to speak of him except in scorn or ridicule,' he writes. To the missionary, on the other hand, the Western lay businessman was 'hard, immoral, addicted to drink, interested only in mulcting wealth from the poor Chinese while arrogantly excluding them from his cities, clubs and vacation spots, and remaining indifferent to both the values and the needs of their indigenous culture'.

There were certain elements of truth here, Gilkey claims, but the picture was wildly exaggerated. The businessman had simply built his own world which he never left; it never seemed to have crossed his mind that he might become part of the wider Chinese culture around him:

> His life was circumscribed by the narrow confines of the business office, the club porch, and the social life among the treaty-port elite. Outside that small circle of foreign equals, there were for him only the Chinese subordinates in his office (whom he did not understand, and so tended to distrust), beyond them the great sea of Chinese 'natives' in whom he had little interest except as a market. In his environment – 'a little bit of Surrey in North China, old boy' – there was no wider community within which he might, as he would at home, adopt a responsible role commensurate with his wealth and advantages.

The merchants' picture of the missionary was the usual stereotype. To the businessman, says Gilkey, the missionary was a loveless, sexless, viceless, disapproving and hypocritical fanatic. He was repressed and repressive, trying to force others into the narrow straitjacket of his own list of rigid 'dos' and 'don'ts' and thus squeezing out of his own life and theirs all its natural and redeeming joys. And Gilkey adds: 'At first, in Peking, I found this picture incredible; it seemed so clearly not to fit the liberal group I knew. But acquaintance in camp with a much wider circle of missionaries showed that it did contain some truth.'

In page after page of Gilkey's account, the missionaries feature in the most unattractive light. He describes how, at the beginning of the camp, the Japanese had put some of the families of four into two rooms, while others were squashed into one room. In an attempt to give the one-roomed families more space, it was suggested that the teenage children of four-person families could be put into a dormitory. With this in mind, Gilkey visited a prominent American missionary family, who had two sons aged sixteen and thirteen, to ask if one or both of the sons might move into a dormitory, thus providing extra room to help the crowded families. The family must have known about the problem, he says, because one of the overcrowded families of four-in-a-room lived right next door. Gilkey records the exchange as he recalls it.

'We have had our evening of thought and prayer about the problem you shared with us,' said the missionary's wife, smiling, 'and we have reached our decision. We cannot allow our young sons to go into the dorm.'

'But they will be only 50 yards away,' said Gilkey. 'Surely you don't think anything will happen to them there?'

'Oh no, it's just that Paul is only sixteen and subject to so many influences right now. I don't want to say anything about those other boys, but you know how they are. And besides, the heating and draughts here are very unusual and I know that, with the little he gets to eat, unless someone watches over him, he will always be getting colds and flu. And it is quite out of the question for Johnny at thirteen to leave us.'

'OK, fair enough,' said Gilkey. 'Let's look at another alternative then. How about your youngest moving into this room with you, and Paul moving in with the two Jones boys in the next block?'

'Oh no, we talked about that, too, and have made up our minds. We believe in keeping a nice home for our boys to come to, and that would be impossible with four in one room. As we talked last night, all this became clearer and clearer: home and family are so important in a place like this. We decided that our first moral responsibility in the camp is to keep a real American home for our two boys.'

Gilkey also reports incidents like the squabble between a fervent missionary and a chic British secretary. 'These ruddy missionaries,' the representative of the secretaries explained, 'insisted not only on praying aloud at night, but on singing hymns when they awoke each morning, God help them, at 6a.m. We finally got damn well tired of this nonsense, and that is the cause of the fight.'

'You know perfectly well it isn't,' retorted an outraged British woman missionary. 'They insisted on chattering endlessly at night in loud whispers when we were trying to sleep, as any normal woman should have been. And not only talking, but talking about all the lurid escapades in their pasts, half of which I am sure were imagined. And that started the fight.'

As a partial solution, the most vociferous hymn-singer was moved into a predominantly missionary dormitory. Annie Buchan, the matron from the Siaochang Mission Hospital who arrived in the camp some months after the others, remembered a similar situation.

'In our dorm there was an old woman, a dear soul. It didn't matter what was happening, her devotions came first. Every morning she would get on her knees on the floor for her devotions. But the person in the next bed had to climb over her to get to her work. That kind of thing went on.' Annie Buchan chuckled. 'It wasn't really necessary to irritate anyone in your devotions. You could just as easily communicate with God in your own bed.'

Gilkey's catalogue of the unattractive behaviour of the missionaries is relentless. He describes how sixteen packets of American cigarettes arrived once in the parcel each person received from the Red Cross. The missionaries were thus faced with the moral problem of what to do with them. Their rigid principle of non-smoking required that they should destroy the cigarettes, but as Gilkey reports: 'It was very tempting to use them… Lucrative deals were now possible, since heavy smokers offered tins of milk, butter and meat in exchange for a pack or two.' He says that almost all those missionaries who had previously refused to lend out their ration cards now exchanged their sixteen packets of cigarettes for tins of milk or meat.

He comments:

> It had long been evident that our community was faced with moral problems deep enough to threaten its very existence. And yet a significantly large group of Christian leaders was concerned exclusively with moral issues and vices not connected with these deeper problems of our life. For this reason their very moral intensity tended to make both themselves, and the serious morality which they represented, seem to be a socially irrelevant segment of life rather than the creative force they might have been. The constructive moral forces in our life were only weakened and the cynical forces strengthened, when missionaries judged honest, hard-working and generally self-sacrificing men as 'weak' – and even went so far as to warn their young people not to associate with them – because they smoked or swore.

In his graphic and disillusioned portraits of the people he remembered, Gilkey used assumed names that are just close enough to the real ones to reveal their true identities. There is scarcely a break in his dismal litany of bickerings and fights, repressive morality and greedy self-seeking. How and where, you begin to wonder, did Eric Liddell fit into all this? After all, these were his people that Gilkey was describing so disapprovingly.

Gilkey moves on to the children of non-missionary parents. Life in camp was grey and boring for them. Youngsters in their early teens wandered round the camp at night with nothing to do, and there were rumours of clandestine sex in a disused basement. Gilkey says that at a mass meeting to discuss this crisis, the parents became irate and declared that 'they', whoever that might be, should do something about it. But not one parent offered any concrete suggestions or constructive help, and it was left to the missionary teachers to suggest a solution. It is at that point in Gilkey's jaundiced account, in which praise is always hedged with reservations and enthusiasm tempered by wariness, that you suddenly come across this:

> The man who more than anyone brought about the solution of the teenage problem was Eric Ridley. It is rare indeed that a person has the good fortune to meet a saint, but he came as close to it as anyone I have ever known. Often in an evening of that last year, I (headed for some pleasant rendezvous with my girlfriend) would pass the games room and peer in to see what the missionaries had going for the teenagers. As often as not, Eric would be bent over a chessboard or a model boat, or directing some sort of square dance – absorbed, weary and interested, pouring all of himself into this effort to capture the minds and imaginations of those penned-up youths. If anyone could have done it, he could. A track man, he had won the 400 metres in the twenties for England, and then had come to China as a missionary. In camp he was in his middle forties, lithe and springy of step and, above all, overflowing with good humour and love of life. He was aided by others, to be sure. But it was Eric's enthusiasm and charm that carried the day with the whole effort.

This is an astonishing tribute from the acerbic Mr Gilkey for the lightly disguised Eric 'Ridley' Liddell. This man, he insists, was distinctively different in every area where some of his fellow missionaries were at their least attractive. He bridged the gulf between the missionaries and the businessmen, and was respected by both. In the Great Cigarette Crisis, he had stood by his principles and destroyed the cigarettes he could otherwise have sold. He prayed privately and quietly. He lived out his morality, thrusting it on nobody. His smile was infectious.

Eric Liddell, of course, was already a celebrity by the time he arrived at the camp. 'Don't stare now,' one internee had whispered to a new arrival as they trudged through the camp, 'but that man coming towards us is Eric Liddell.' The newcomer remembered the occasion for a long time:

I was too limp to connect the oncoming stranger with the well-known
Olympic athlete of some years before, but I glanced aside to note the man
on the path. He was not very tall, rather thin, very bronzed with sun and
air. He was wearing the most comical shirt I had ever seen, though I was
to get accustomed to similar garments in that place. It was made, I learned
later, from a pair of Mrs Liddell's curtains.

The Chefoo youngsters were particularly impressed at finding a sporting
hero in their midst. In his book, *A Boy's War*, David Michell remembers
that he and another schoolboy were playing conkers with acorns sus-
pended on a piece of string when his companion looked up and said,
'Do you know who that is coming up the camp road?' Walking towards
them with a springy step, says Michell, was 'a strong, athletic-looking
man in baggy shorts down to his knees and a shirt made out of curtain
material.' His friend enlightened him.

'That's Eric Liddell the Olympic gold medallist who wouldn't run
on a Sunday.'

Michell recalls that although Liddell was already well known, he didn't
rest on his laurels but carried heavy responsibilities and was 'an outstanding example by his kindness and self-sacrifice.'

People frequently smiled at his taste for colourful shirts. But if there
was one satisfaction that Eric discovered in Weihsien camp it was being
able to indulge his passion for garish garments without anyone disapproving. Flo's curtains were nothing special among an exotic array of
clothing that comprised everything from school uniforms to tattered fur
coats. One lady who arrived at the camp took one look at the crowd of
people at the gate and thought they were insane. They were bleary-eyed
and haggard, their clothes a pathetic echo of the different lifestyles from
which they had been snatched.

When Eric first arrived in the camp he was immediately assigned to
the school as a maths and science teacher. He was also put in charge
of camp sports, which involved not only whipping up enthusiasm and
rounding people up for teams, but looking after all the equipment. He
would tear up curtains, sheets and tablecloths of his own to mend hockey
sticks in winter and sew up baseballs in summer.

He also acted as warden of Blocks 23 and 24, two large buildings
housing 230 unattached men and women, boys and girls. It was his job
to collect supplies and make sure all his charges were in place at the
roll-call every morning and evening. With those in the room he had
to share such daily duties as fetching water, dumping dirty water and

rubbish and cleaning the room. In the evenings he tutored youngsters who wanted to keep up their studies in camp. He was also put in charge of the Weihsien Christian Fellowship. Yet another of his jobs was that of chief translator for the Japanese in the camp. These were his official tasks. But you would also see him around the camp mending a hockey stick here, carrying coal for an old person there, bent over some game to keep a youngster amused, helping a child with her books. 'Really he was without a doubt the person most in demand and most respected and loved in camp,' said one former internee. 'One night he was telling us at our place how many hours he figured he did a week, and I was amazed that anyone could carry such a timetable.'

The games that Langdon Gilkey had seen him organising included chess and draughts tournaments, craft shows, dart contests, one-act plays and homemade puppet shows. The trouble with the teenagers never recurred after this programme was arranged for them. It ought to be mentioned that Eric was not alone in his work with these young children. It was teachers like him from among the easily maligned missionaries who devised the programme of games and entertainments while the parents did nothing. It was they who gave up their free time to keep the youngsters amused. The missionaries were also among the group who eventually solved the toilet problem. Along with a number of Catholic priests and nuns, they tied cloths round their faces, borrowed boots and mops and tackled the horrendous job of unstopping the toilets. They then prevented a recurrence of the problem by suggesting that inmates should flush the toilets after each use with a half-bucket of water.

For all the criticisms he had of some of them, the missionaries win a rare tribute from Gilkey in the end. He writes:

> There was a quality seemingly unique to the missionary group, namely, naturally and without pretence to respond to a need which everyone else recognised only to turn aside. Much of this went unnoticed, but our camp could scarcely have survived as well as it did without it. If there were any evidences of the grace of God observable on the surface of our camp existence, they were to be found here.

The many former internees who remember Eric Liddell at that camp offer vivid, affectionate accounts of the things they used to find him doing. One wrote:

Eric taught when he could. He coached boys and girls hoping to specialise in university when the time for release came. For one girl alone he made a beautiful notebook full of drawings of apparatus which she ought to have been using, but could not, and with that to guide her she did learn enough later to enter Melbourne University straight from the camp when the war was over.

Besides this work, he organised all the games. Evening after evening he tore up, with a grim smile, all of the sheets his wife had left for his use, just to bind up the injured blades of the few precious hockey-sticks which had somehow made their way into internment with us. He gummed the strips of linen with Chinese glue melted down over a one-candle-power peanut-oil lamp. He took over the 'prepites' of Chefoo school... so that their weary teacher could put her feet up for a few precious minutes once a week.

It was fun to see him teaching them rounders. He arranged for the Americans to run a series of baseball matches, though he took no responsibility for any Sunday games, which they asked for... To encourage the eighteen-year-old lads to keep fit, he would run the circumference of the camp within the walls and teach them something of running techniques.

This was not all his work by any means. He was on the Camp Discipline Committee, a most important organisation of our own which prevented many a silly scrape from getting to the ears of the Japanese guards. He also taught Bible class on Sundays. Most of all he was the man we turned to when personal relationships got just too impossible. We lived in large dormitories with but six feet by three feet of space for ourselves and what belongings we had. He had a gentle, humorous way of soothing ruffled tempers and bringing to one's mind some bygone happiness or the prospect of some future interest round the corner 'when we got out'.

In a camp rife with back-biting and gossip, there was no one who had a bad word to say of Eric Liddell. His attitude to everyone was the same. You would find him talking to the businessman just the same way as to the Roman Catholic priest or the child from Chefoo. There is something immensely touching about the tributes to his life from this period, something about the kind of details they all remember, that leaps out with the force of truth. For instance, there is the story of how he had his Edinburgh presentation gold watch carefully weighed and valued, because there was a shortage of softball gear and money was needed to buy more. The sacrifice was not required in the end, because money came in at the last minute. But the gesture was noticed.

It is fascinating to talk to people who were youngsters at the time and listen to them thinking aloud about the man whom every child in the camp knew. Isabel Harris came to Weihsien from Chefoo school as a fourteen-year-old. As Mrs Isabel Herron, she spoke from her Edinburgh home of the impact he had made on her:

> My memory of Eric is at the side of the hockey field, examining all our sticks as we came off. We didn't have a chance of replacing a stick then; it had to go on being mended and mended. And I remember Eric taking the sticks away and meticulously binding them up and always having them ready for the next game. He never seemed to be too busy. He was always around helping us.
>
> I remember him being angry on the hockey pitch with someone for playing foul or something. If you felt you had done something wrong then you would probably hear from him. He was a friend; someone around if you needed him. He used to spend a lot of time carrying water for infirm people and carrying coal. He wasn't a very good preacher, but he certainly had us all there listening to him just because his personality, or his sincerity, or whatever it was, came across so strongly.
>
> When Eric died, one of the women in the camp, a Russian prostitute, told my mother that Eric Liddell was the only man who had ever done anything for her and not wanted to be repaid in kind. I think that when she first moved into camp he'd gone and put some shelves up for her. She was a woman living on her own, she didn't have anyone to do that kind of thing. And it didn't matter what walk of life a person came from, Eric wouldn't judge anybody. There were missionaries in the camp who wouldn't have helped someone like her, but Eric didn't see things that way.
>
> He would do anything rather than talk about his Olympic feat: not through false modesty, but he was too interested in the present. He wasn't particularly interested in the past. It was one very important part of his life, but I think there were also some equally important parts of his life.
>
> It's hard to explain, but missionaries can be people who keep themselves so much apart. There were some people who were more interested in, how shall I say, their own kind, and not so interested in others. And missionaries who didn't really have time for these other people's children, and just worked with the missionaries' children. But Eric worked right across the board with everyone. It keeps on coming across in my memory of him. He must have been very strong, because he really did treat us all the same.

Another Chefoo child, Norman Cliff, wrote a book of his camp experiences, *Courtyard of the Happy Way*. There he calls Eric Liddell 'the most outstanding Weihsien personality... in his early forties, quiet-spoken and with a permanent smile. Eric was the finest Christian man I have ever had the privilege of meeting.'

What these people keep coming back to, again and again, is the way Liddell lived his Christianity. Here at the camp he is being portrayed as the Christ-figure just as much as he was among the Chinese in Siaochang. He befriends the prostitute and the despised businessman; he carries coal for the weak and teaches the young; he prepares to sell his gold watch and tears up his sheets for hockey sticks. And yet he is still the same Eric, striding around in a multi-coloured shirt made out of old curtains and looking extremely ordinary and nothing special at all.

One of the hardest decisions he had to make in the camp was what to do about Sunday games. No, he said, there were to be no games on Sundays; it was a principle from which he had never deviated. But many of the teenagers protested against the Sabbath ban and decided to organise a hockey game by themselves – boys against girls. Without a referee it ended in a free fight. On the following Sunday, Eric quietly turned out to act as referee. It is a most illuminating detail of his life: he would not run on a Sunday for an Olympic gold medal and all the glory in the world; but he refereed a game on a Sunday, breaking his unbreakable principle, just to keep a handful of imprisoned youngsters at peace with each other.

From time to time Eric preached at church services in the camp, and his subject was nearly always the Sermon on the Mount, or St Paul's hymn of love in 1 Corinthians. 'Though I speak with the tongues of men and of angels and have not love,' he would tell his listeners, 'I am become as sounding brass or a tinkling cymbal.' These words of St Paul were the cornerstone of his faith, as was Christ's Sermon on the Mount: blessed are the poor in spirit, the mourners, the meek, the merciful, the pure in heart, the peacemakers, the persecuted. This was the way he believed love could be translated into living.

He had once written a little booklet called *The Sermon on the Mount: For Sunday School Teachers*. It was published as he left Tientsin to begin his work out in the country in 1937. In it Eric had encapsulated his years of study and insight. At one point he notes:

'Blessed are the meek: for they shall inherit the earth', St Matthew 5:5 (see Psalm 37,11). Meek — Gentle of temper, humble, kind, mild, yielding, unassuming. Note Aristotle's account of it as the character of one who has the passion of resentment under control, and who is therefore tranquil and untroubled. Control because of clear conscience. Meekness and weakness often associated together. What is the difference? Both may be kind and gentle. Is the difference the element of fear?

Meek — kind and gentle and fearless.

Weak — kind and gentle and led by fear.

Meek — is love in the presence of wrong.

In another book, *Prayers for Daily Use,* published in 1942 in the period before internment, he wrote about obedience as the key to knowing God: 'OBEDIENCE to God's will is the secret of spiritual knowledge and insight. It is not willingness to know, but willingness to DO (obey) God's Will that brings certainty.'

These were the subjects he talked about in the camp services, both on the communal church occasions and in smaller evening meetings. It was always the same: love and obedience and the fragrance of a God-enfolded life. Sometimes he illustrated his points with his own sporting memories. On one Tuesday evening in 1944, as part of a series of Whitsuntide talks, he told them this story:

Several years ago I sat in the grandstand at a great sports meeting where the finest athletes of the USA and the British Empire met in competition. There was an obstacle race in which competitors had to run round the course many times, jumping hurdles as they went. After several rounds the competitors were fairly well separated, except for the first two who were running within ten years of each other.

As the first man took one of the hurdles, his foot struck the top of it and knocked it over. The blow was not hard enough to affect him much, a slight stagger and on he went. The fallen hurdle left a gap. It gave the second man the chance to run through the gap instead of taking a jump and thus gain a slight advantage.

Ten yards behind means less than two seconds. In the fraction of a second at his disposal a decision was made. He swerved to the side, jumped the hurdle next to the fallen one and then moved back in to the edge of the track again.

I can remember the thrill that went through me, and the answering cheer that rose from the crowd. That was the finest thing done that day.

He did not win; I have forgotten who did, but I can never forget that action. He could not act otherwise. He was let by the Spirit of Sportsmanship. It was ingrained in him, part of himself.

Eric Liddell.

Sport is wonderful. The most wonderful part of it is not the almost superhuman achievements but the spirit in which it is done. Take away that spirit and it is dead.

The Holy Spirit is to the Christian life what sportsmanship is to sport and more. Without Him in our lives, even at the best, we are little better than Tennyson's Maud:

Perfectly beautiful: let it be granted her; where is the fault?

All that I saw (for her eyes were downcast, not to be seen)

Faultily faultless, icily regular, splendidly null

Dead perfection and no more.

As always, those who listened to Eric Liddell were mesmerised by something they found difficult to define: 'his personality, or his sincerity, or whatever it was', as Isabel Herron rather helplessly tried to express it. What was his secret? People were asking it then as some are still asking today.

Another internee came up with her own answer:

> What was his secret? Once I asked him, but I really knew already, for my husband was in his dormitory and shared the secret with him. Every morning about 6a.m., with curtains tightly drawn to keep in the shining of our peanut-oil lamp, lest the prowling sentries would think someone was trying to escape, he used to climb out of his top bunk, past the sleeping forms of his dormitory mates. Then, at the small Chinese table, the two men would sit close together with the light just enough to illumine their Bibles and notebooks. Silently they read, prayed, thought about the day's duties, noted what should be done. Eric was a man of prayer not only at set times – though he did not like to miss a prayer meeting or communion service when such could be arranged. He talked to God all the time, naturally, as one can who enters the 'school of prayer' to learn this way of inner discipline. He seemed to have no weighty mental problems: his life was grounded in God, in faith, and in trust.

But the strains of camp life were gradually taking their toll on the internees, particularly those over forty. There were mental breakdowns and cases of typhoid, malaria and dysentery. The heat could be unbearable and, hardest to bear, supplies of food grew more and more meagre as 1944 drew to an end. Eric, too, was feeling the strain.

When Annie Buchan arrived at Weihsien several months after him, she noticed a difference in his appearance. 'What's happened to Eric? He's slowed down. He's walking slowly, he's talking slowly,' she went round saying to people. No one else in the camp had noticed any change in him; it took the eye of someone who had known him for years but had not seen him for a long time to realise that Eric had lost his bounce and spring.

The former matron of the Siaochang Hospital had originally thought she was going to escape internment. She had been given a card from the authorities saying that because she had been 'humane', she would be exempt. But one day, Japanese guards came and told her she must leave the British Consulate in Peking, where she had been nursing an invalid friend until the lady's death. She was to go to Weihsien as an act of reprisal: two men had escaped from the camp, and she was to be interned in their place.

She found that Eric, whom she had not seen for some years, was doing far too much work:

Eric had a very heavy responsibility. More than he should have had, I think. But people depended on him so much. He was teaching science to the children from Chefoo, and that was enough for him alone. But he was so willing that he was doing a lot of odd jobs for people. They depended on him to organise all the camp entertainments. There were other teachers there who could have done it, but Eric was always there. It was too much.

By the autumn of 1944, Eric was losing some of his resilience; he was also feeling the strain of being separated for so long from his family. Some of the internees were surprised to discover later that he had a wife and family at all, because he so rarely complained of missing them. 'There were other people in the same position,' Isabel Herron said, 'who went round moaning that they had not seen their wives. But Eric was so busy cheering other people up that he kept his own miseries and problems very much to himself. He was a very private person. I remember being quite surprised at finding out how close he and Flo actually were.'

By this time, after eighteen months of internment, even Eric's phenomenal energy had been sapped by privation and hunger. The constant games-playing for the benefit of the youngsters was particularly tiring. The inhabitants of Weihsien internment camp, without knowing it, were slowly starving. Had it not been for the arrival of Red Cross parcels at the end of January 1945, they would all have been in desperate trouble.

Eric never complained about the conditions, or his health. But he made no attempt to hide his private feelings from Annie Buchan, who knew him so well. Whenever the pair had any spare time, they would go and sit in the open courtyard and out would come Eric's snapshots of Florence and the children. Poring over the photographs, Eric would give her any news he had had from Canada, which was usually very little, because letters were taking months to arrive. In one of these quiet talks he told her something she has never forgotten: 'My big worry, Annie,' he said, 'is that I didn't give Flo enough of my time.' One day he alarmed her by saying he could not see any future – everything seemed blank. 'And that wasn't like Eric,' said Annie. 'He had always been full of hope.'

In the middle of January 1945 Eric, who was suffering already from incipient malnutrition like everyone else in the camp, had an attack of what was thought to be influenza with severe sinusitis; but the serious inflammation did not respond to treatment as readily as it should have done. He suffered from agonising headaches, and would lie in his room with his eyes bandaged, wanting nothing but quiet.

As soon as Annie Buchan heard that he was ill, she marched directly to the men's dormitory to see him in defiance of the camp rules:

> As soon as I had seen him I went straight to the head doctor at the camp, and said Eric must be brought to hospital. He said there was no room. I said I thought Eric must have hospital treatment. So he was brought in. But he was so courageous, he would never say what he felt was wrong with him; so they just said, 'Oh, he'll get over it.'

In hospital he had what was thought to be a partial stroke. While he was recovering from that, the few visitors he was allowed reported that he seemed bright but occasionally 'wandered', and sounded distressed about his family in Canada. He had a strange look in one eye and spoke haltingly; he had difficulty in walking, for his right leg was partially paralysed. But he remained cheerful, and people who went to see him came away cheered in turn. He talked to one young couple about their approaching marriage; he even discussed the bridesmaid's dress.

The doctors were worried about him, and suspected a brain tumour. They held long and earnest consultations, but with the equipment at their disposal in the camp there was little they could do. Since apart from anything else he was suffering from both nervous and physical exhaustion, a period of complete rest was prescribed.

For a time he seemed to rally, and started moving about again. However, he was still getting these piercing pains in his head. When a solicitous friend asked if his head were any better, he replied, 'To answer that question I'd need to know what is going on inside my head.' He told a veteran missionary colleague from Siaochang, C.H.B. Longman, that the doctor thought he had had a nervous breakdown. The pain in his head had been causing him bouts of depression for some time; but what concerned him more was that he felt it was a sign of spiritual weakness in himself that he could not bear everything as cheerfully as he would have liked, in faith. 'There is just one thing that troubles me,' he told a fellow missionary in his slow, limping speech. 'I ought to have been able to cast it all on the Lord, and not to have broken under it.'

For a while, however, he seemed to be on the mend. He was allowed out to have tea with his friends. He even insisted on climbing four flights of stairs to visit a colleague in his room in the top storey of the hospital block. 'It was like reaching for the stars,' said the nurse who helped him; but he made it.

On the last day of his life he went out for a stroll in the afternoon. Near the hospital he stopped to speak to a group of boys beside the open space where he had taught them to play basketball and rounders. David Michell recalls sadly: 'As usual he was smiling. As he talked to us, we knew nothing of the pain he was hiding, and he knew nothing of the brain tumour that was to take his life that evening.'

Eric also met the wife of one of his Tientsin colleagues. They walked for about fifteen minutes and she too thought he seemed his usual cheerful self again.

'Have you heard from Flo?' she asked him.

Yes, he'd had one of her letters, he said. He seemed tired, and spoke haltingly.

'You ought to be resting more,' she said.

'No, I must get my walking legs again,' he replied.

Eric might have been on his way to the post office to send his last letter to his wife. It was dated the same day, 21 February 1945, but typed rather than written by hand, which suggests that someone else had written it for him. The Japanese allowed the internees only 100 words per letter, so they had to write in a kind of telegraphese. Florence only received it several months later and was hugely disturbed to realise how ill and unlike himself Eric must have been feeling despite the brave words:

> Was carrying too much responsibility. Slight nervous breakdown. Am much better after month's rest in hospital. Doctor suggests changing my work. Giving up teaching and taking up physical work like baking. A good change. So glad to get your letter of July. Mrs. Longman is much better. Bear and Nelma making preparations for marriage on April 18. Will send particulars later. Wish you could enter into the celebrations. Joyce Stranks has been a great help to me in hospital, keeping me in touch with the news. Enjoying comfort parcels. Special love to yourself and the children. – Eric.

At some point during the afternoon he also wrote down some phrases from his favourite hymn, 'Be Still, My Soul.' Twenty years earlier he had written to Florence during their engagement: 'I often play it over. It goes to the beautiful tune, *Finlandia* – a calm, restful, beautiful tune.' A few days previously he had asked the Salvation Army Band, who used to play hymns outside the hospital every Sunday afternoon, to play 'Be Still, My Soul' for him. Norman Cliff, one of the Chefoo youngsters, was a second trombonist in the band (led by Salvationist Fred Buist but ecumenical in its camp membership) and he remembers playing outside the hospital on the day that the nurse on duty passed a note out of the window, which read: 'Eric Liddell would like you to play *Finlandia*.'

'We gladly obliged,' said Cliff. As they played it, he was thinking of the words of Katherina von Schlegel's eighteenth century hymn:

> Be still, my soul. The Lord is on thy side;
> Bear patiently the cross of grief or pain.
> Leave to thy God to order and provide;
> In every change He faithful will remain.
> Be still, my soul – thy best, thy heavenly Friend
> Through thorny ways leads to a joyful end.

Eric himself must have been mulling it over again on the afternoon of his death, for he wrote the words 'Be still, my soul' on a piece of paper, along with other broken phrases from the hymn.

That evening he had a spasm of choking and coughing. Seventeen-year-old Joyce Stranks, whom Eric had been coaching in chemistry and softball, was with him at the time, and he clutched her arm as the pain seized him. Then the spasm passed, and later in the evening he was laughing and joking again with one of the missionaries' children. Suddenly he took another attack. Joyce ran out and called for the doctor, who had him moved to a separate and single room.

There, Annie Buchan, who had just come off nursing duty, came to his bedside:

> I asked him how he was feeling, and he said no one had a clue what was wrong. That was the phrase he used: 'They haven't a clue.' After that I simply refused to leave. I stayed. One or two of the doctors were standing in the middle of the ward next door and talking about Eric, and I just went in to them and said, 'Do you realise Eric is dying?' Somebody said, 'Nonsense.' I went back into Eric's room, and by this time Eric was pretty far through. And he just said to me, 'Annie, it's complete surrender.' Then he took a convulsion and vomited all over me, and then he was gone into a coma and he never recovered.
>
> 'Surrender.' Yes, that's what he said. I was holding him. I could hardly hear him. He started saying it. He could hardly get the words out, but he definitely said 'complete surrender'.

They were words that had often been on Eric Liddell's lips. His life had been lived in the spirit of absolute surrender to God; now, at the end, he gave himself finally. As Annie Buchan said with a smile, 'Eric had been surrendering to God all his life through. I don't believe it cost him much to say "complete surrender", because he knew where he was going.'

The next day an autopsy revealed an inoperable tumour on the left side of his brain. It was this that had caused the agony of the preceding weeks, and the massive haemorrhage that eventually killed him.

11

'There's No Way Anyone Like Him Could Die'

On the snowy February day after Eric died, Weihsien internment camp was cold and numb with shock. Hardly anyone had known he was ill, and the end had come with horrifying swiftness.

'I can just remember the shock going through the camp,' said Isabel Herron. '"It can't be true," we were saying. "There's no way that anyone like him could die."'

Langdon Gilkey reports: 'The entire camp, especially its youth, was stunned for days, so great was the vacuum that Eric's death had left.'

On Saturday 24 February, they held his funeral. It was a bleak wind-swept day. People from all over the camp crowded into the hall for the service, and those who couldn't get in stood outside. The numbers waiting in the cold outside the hall were an unprecedented tribute. For the first time missionaries and city businessmen mingled in fellowship, their presence together an unspoken testimony. There must have been at least one person there from most of the twenty-one nationalities in the camp. People who would never have been expected to attend were there, people whom one would think had nothing in common with the things Eric Liddell stood for. And many were in tears.

Those inside waited in silence while the music of 'I Know that My Redeemer Liveth' on the piano sounded round the hall. The table was piled high with wreaths: from missionary colleagues; from the men in his dormitory and the people he had supervised as warden; from the Boy Scouts and Girl Guides whom he had helped keep going as an organisation in the camp; from the children of the Weihsien School; from the officers of the Salvation Army.

One of the senior missionaries, the Revd Dr Arnold Bryson, gave a short address, the first of a long stream of tributes to Eric Liddell in the months to come that would have made him shrivel with embarrassment:

Although his activities lay chiefly in the religious, athletic and educational departments of camp life, his genial, winsome disposition and his readiness to help anyone in need attracted both young and old. From his humble and modest demeanour no one could have guessed that here was a man with an international reputation on the running track and football field.

The sudden removal of such a man in the prime of his life, and at the peak of his powers, inevitably raises questions in our hearts. Why did God take him from a world in which such men are so sorely needed today? But God makes no mistakes. His thoughts are not our thoughts, neither are His ways our ways. Perhaps in God's loving purpose, by Eric's early promotion to higher service he was spared years of acute suffering, and we can only bow to God's will.

Yesterday a man said to me, 'Of all the men I have known, Eric Liddell was the one in whose character and life the spirit of Jesus Christ was pre-eminently manifested.' And all of us who were privileged to know him with any intimacy echo this judgement. What was the secret of his consecrated life and far-reaching influence? Absolute surrender to God's will as revealed in Jesus Christ. His was a God-controlled life and he followed his Master and Lord with a devotion that never flagged and with an intensity of purpose that made men see both the reality and power of true religion.

After a prayer, a hymn, the Lord's Prayer, the Benediction and a closing voluntary, 'O Rest in the Lord', the funeral service was over. Then the coffin was borne by his friends through a guard of honour, composed of the children from the Chefoo and the Weihsien schools, to the quiet cemetery in the Japanese officers' headquarters where several other internees were buried. Among the pall-bearers was eighteen-year-old Stephen Metcalf, who would return sixty years later to pay tribute to Liddell at this same spot. As he bore the coffin in the biting cold, he glanced at the old bound-up running shoes which Eric had given him only weeks earlier to see him through the winter.

At the windy graveside the funeral party repeated the Beatitudes from the Sermon on the Mount that had been Eric Liddell's special inspiration. 'Blessed are the meek; for they shall inherit the earth,' they chorused, as the wind lifted their hair and tugged at their coats. 'Blessed are the pure in heart; for they shall see God. Blessed are the peacemakers; for they shall be called the children of God.' Then his body was lowered into the grave.

On 3 March, the big Edwardian-style church at the camp was filled to overflowing for a memorial service conducted by Eric's old friend, schoolmaster, colleague and flatmate, A.P. Cullen. The melody of Sibelius' beautiful *Finlandia* reduced many to tears as they sang 'Be Still, My Soul', the hymn Eric had loved best. But it was comforting, too, with its implicit reminder of Psalm 46 and the command, in the midst of life's trials, to 'Be still and know that I am God.' The congregation stayed in their seats and sang it very quietly and softly. Today there are still people all over the world who think instantly of Eric Liddell whenever they hear the strains of that hymn, and are carried back to a church in an internment camp in China all those years ago.

'I always associate him with "Be still, my soul; the Lord is on thy side",' said one former Chefoo schoolgirl. 'I think it's because I remember him as such a still, serene person. When I heard that hymn at the service that day, I felt things were going to turn out all right in the end.'

Talking about funerals once, Eric told Flo that he would come back and haunt her if she ever allowed any of the eulogies that always made him so uncomfortable. But Florence Liddell, still blissfully unaware on the other side of the world that her husband was dead, could take no part in deciding the content of the Weihsien memorial service. And who, in any case, would have had the heart to stop his friends saying what they were all aching to express that day? A.P. Cullen told the huge gathering:

> I have known Eric for thirty-three years, since he was a schoolboy of ten at Eltham College. I have been in frequent contact with him for the last twenty years. After his family left for Canada, he and I lived together, just the two of us, in my flat till January 1942. From then until he came here fourteen months later, almost every day I went for a long walk with him. And from my knowledge of him, gained in this close association over many years, I say that Eric is the most remarkable example in my experience of a man of average ability and talents developing those talents to an amazing degree, and even appearing to acquire new talents from time to time, through the power of the Holy Spirit. He was, literally, God-controlled, in his thought, judgement, actions, words, to an extent I have never seen surpassed, and rarely seen equalled.

He described the regular and rapid progress of Eric's spiritual development as being:

> as phenomenal as the speed with which, in a 100 yards race, after being yards behind at half-way, he would catch up and pass the winning-post

an easy first, leaving the other competitors standing… Indeed, the growth of his spiritual life affords a remarkable parallel to his methods of running a race, for one of the astonishing things in his victories on the track… was that he was always a bit slow in getting off the mark, mainly, I am convinced, because his fine conscience would never allow him to 'beat the gun'.

Then he spoke about the word which had been Eric's last: surrender:

Let us now turn to the way in which he tried to work out that ideal. First of all, absolute surrender to the will of God. Absolute surrender – those words were often on his lips, the conception was always in his mind; that God should have absolute control over every part of his life. It was towards the attainment of that ideal that he directed all his mental and spiritual energies.

W.E. McLaren, a shipping agent in Tientsin, who had played threequarter beside Eric as a rugby international for Scotland, spoke of Liddell the sportsman: 'Many a time he was lain for by his opponents, whose tactics were at least doubtful, but never would he repay them in their own coin. His method was invariable – he merely played better rugby and made them look like second-raters.'

But perhaps the most remarkable and honest tribute was one that was not made in public, but in private. It was confided to a day-to-day diary that was kept throughout the vicissitudes and sorrows of those months in captivity:

February 24. Eric's funeral today.

He was not particularly clever, and not conspicuously able, but he was good.

He was naturally reserved and tended to live in a world of his own, but he gave of himself unstintedly.

He always shrank from revealing his deepest needs and distresses, so that while he bore the burdens of many, very few could help to bear his.

His fame as an athlete helped him a good deal. He certainly didn't look like a great runner, but the fact that he had been one gave him a self-confidence that men of his type don't have.

He wasn't a great leader, or an inspired thinker, but he knew what he ought to do, and he did it.

He was a true disciple of the Master and worthy of the highest places amongst the saints.

On 2 May 1945, more than two months after Eric's death, two family friends arrived at 21, Gloucester Street, Toronto, the home of Florence Liddell's parents, where she and the three children were staying.

Speaking in 1981, Florence described what happened the day she learned she was a widow:

I invited them in and I sensed there was something wrong. So finally I said to them, 'Have you got bad news? Is it one of the boys?' (I had two brothers, you know.) Even then it never crossed my mind that it would be Eric.

About a month before this visit, I had had the strangest feeling. I was standing at the stove and I thought, 'If you turn round, Eric is standing there.' I could just feel vibrations. He was so full of life and bouncy. And he said, 'It's OK, Flossie. Everything is going to be all right.' (Flossie is the name he always used to tease me; it used to make me mad.) I thought my nerves were going. For three weeks I was conscious of his presence in this way. But it never crossed my mind that he had died. I am sure that somehow or other he was allowed to come back.

I was terribly crushed when I got the news. I was all for jumping off the bridge. But again his influence was just there; as if he were saying, 'Florence, what are you going to accomplish by jumping off the bridge?' I was thinking I would catch up with Eric that way, but he would just look at me as if to say, 'Flo, what about the three little girls I've left in your care?' And that stopped me.

I had had no hint that he was even ill. Three or four Red Cross letters from him came after I heard he was dead, and one mentioned that he was in hospital and that they thought he might be working too hard. He got these terrible headaches at that time and he got depressed because he had always thought his faith would carry him through. A couple from the Salvation Army wrote to me afterwards and said they had seen him putting his hand to the wall to steady himself sometimes. That's when I really felt bad.

He had told me nothing about what life was like in the camp. He just talked about the children and said he was helping with the sports. They had to be very circumspect in their letters. Generally, on the back of the letter form there was a space where you could reply; and it would take from six months to a year for a letter to go back and forwards.

On 11 May, a few days after hearing the news about her husband's death, Florence wrote a letter to Thomas Cocker-Brown, foreign secretary of the London Missionary Society, in which she described in more detail her powerful sense of Eric's presence in the previous few weeks:

> My first reaction was, 'That is why he has been so near me lately.' I have dreamt more about Eric in the last few weeks than I have all the rest of the time I have been home. Every time (in the dreams) he was here we were all terribly happy and everything was so vivid. My reaction was 'That is just wishful thinking getting the better of you.'
>
> Then in making plans for the summer and autumn I seemed to come up against a stone wall. Plans that seemed excellent at first seemed to get blocked. I don't know when I have been so conscious of a restraining hand and I simply couldn't understand it. I felt sure there was going to be some change in plans but I couldn't see what.
>
> The thought flashed into my mind, 'Could it be that Eric is really coming home and we may have to go over to England to meet him? No, that's wishful thinking again.' Never once did I have any premonition of this and even after I knew, I was so vividly conscious of Eric being happy. I could just see his sunny smile and twinkling eyes.
>
> It has been a strange and wonderful experience. At times I have been numbed and overwhelmed by a sense of unreality – of pain – of fear for the future and then there has come welling up from within that power of faith which has carried me through. My faith has been wonderfully strengthened. In looking back I have so much to be thankful for. God has provided so wonderfully – we have been so happy and I know that He is working out his purpose and that good can come out of even this.

After speaking of her gratitude for the kindness and thoughtfulness of her immediate family and friends, she added: ' I feel that Eric and I had as much happiness in our few short years together as many couples have in a whole lifetime and I thank God for the privilege of being Eric's wife.'

Like so many young women confronted with sudden wartime widowhood, Florence also faced a mountain of practical problems. She tackled these with a typically uncomplaining gutsiness which is evident from a second, more businesslike letter she sent to Mr Cocker-Brown on the same day, detailing her financial situation.

Clearly concerned about making ends meet, she wrote that she understood that the LMS would continue to pay an allowance for six months after the husband's death but wondered if that meant six months from 21 February or six months from 3 May, the day after she was notified. She was also worried about whether she qualified for a pension, as Eric had not actually joined the LMS until his first furlough.

Another concern was that Eric had left two small insurance policies, but the one she was looking at now was made out to his estate and not in her name. This reflected a problem she had just discovered with Eric's will:

> Just before leaving Tientsin I went with Eric to the Mission Safe to get all our various papers and certificates, etc. We thought everything was in order but when I open the envelope marked his will, we find it is one he made out before we were married and definitely states is null and void when he marries.
>
> I know he made another will because I saw it and simply can't understand how this had happened. By some fluke we must have destroyed the second one and kept this one. It's most unlike Eric. At first it didn't worry me because outside of the insurance there is absolutely no property and belongings to worry about. But I know nothing about English law and when the policy is made out to the estate and I have no will to show what happens.
>
> I am terribly sorry to trouble you with all this but I didn't know what else to do.

There is something very moving about the way this young woman, still just thirty-three years old, faced up to what had just been thrust upon her. With three young children, barely any income and even the modest insurance policies in doubt because of the loss of Eric's will (had the growing brain tumour perhaps already begun to affect his judgement as early as 1941, when his family left Tientsin?), she showed herself to be gracious, positive and practical. She ends her letter to Cocker-Brown: 'It is quite obvious I will have to go back to nursing but I am very thankful to be young and strong and to have a profession behind me. However with the three children to think of, I'll have to get moving on plans at once.'

This she did, and she brought her daughters up in the kind of home that she and Eric had long planned for them, full of laughter and singing and prayer.

In 1951, six years after Eric's death, Florence remarried. Their eldest daughter Patricia was sixteen by then. Florence's second husband wa a cousin, a Canadian cattle farmer called Murray Hall, with whom she had a happy marriage until his death in 1969. She inherited three step-children, and together they had a seventh child, Jeannie, who was born in 1955. Patricia, Heather and Maureen went on to produce nine grandchildren, seven boys and two girls.

Florence's two husbands were very different kinds of men. Her second husband was a more rough-and-ready sort of man than Eric, she said: 'But we had a very good marriage. I said when Eric died that I would never marry again for security, only for love – and I never thought that would happen. But I found it was possible to love like that again.'

Florence was talking just after the film *Chariots of Fire* had burst on to cinema screens across the world. She spoke with infectious warmth of her life with Eric. Grey-haired, a little stout and walking with some difficulty, her eyes still sparkled with merriment. She mused in her mellow Canadian accent:

> Eric was ten years older than me, you know. I'd like to have seen what he looked like today. He was eternally young, even though he had very little hair. He used to make jokes about it, but his mother was very perturbed and swore it was because he took too many showers.
>
> I liked the way they portrayed him in the film. It was just exactly Eric. It moved me very much. I especially liked the way they had him in Paris telling the Prince of Wales he would not run on a Sunday. The way he was so quiet but stood up for himself and firmly answered back.
>
> He certainly threw himself into his running, didn't he? The way he threw his head back – it was so ridiculous! Boy, I couldn't understand how he could even see. When I ever asked him he just said, 'I knew where I was going all right.' He had the most beautiful laugh.
>
> I consider myself privileged to have been married to him. We were only married eleven years, and for four of these we were separated. But I learned so much from him. It was a super marriage.

Florence died herself on 14 June 1984.

★ ★ ★

Six months after Eric's death, on 17 August 1945, the morning peace of the Weihsien camp was broken by the deafening roar of aircraft overhead. 'J Day had passed two days earlier with no break in camp routine or any indication that relations with the Japanese might have changed. But now the cry went up, 'American plane! American plane!' and hope surged in every man, woman and child in the place. Children in the middle of their weekly singing lesson in the church raced outside and joined a stream of internees pouring out of the shacks all round the compound and making for the athletics field.

There they saw a huge B-24 wheeling in the sky, flying lower and lower until the people waving frantically below could make out its name, The Armoured Angel. At any moment they expected the Japanese on the ground to open fire, but the guns were silent. Lower it came and lower, until slowly it started to move upwards again, and away. The watchers held their breath. Was it going to leave them after all?

In *A Boy's War* David Michell recalls what happened next, a moment of exhilarating joy that etched itself on his young memory for ever:

> To the piercing shrieks and wild cries of everyone, seven GIs parachuted down, floating out of the sky like saviours from another world. Nothing could stop us now. The forbidding gray walls and massive gates in an instant lost their terror. Not even the guards with their bayonets drawn as they stood in line could block our headlong stampede. Some of us children, barefoot and dressed only in shorts, were first down the cinder road to the main gate. We hesitated only momentarily as we neared the soldiers. The shouts and cheers behind us and the hope of deliverance within reach took away our fears. As we surged through the gates with spirits bursting for freedom from the years of imprisonment, the guards fell away to the sides.

The GIs were soon surrounded. One was seized by a woman who hugged and kissed him before fainting in his arms 'Hey, you guys, take this dame off my neck,' he roared to his fellow parachutists. All seven were then grabbed and hoisted on to the shoulders of some of the male prisoners, who paraded them through the gates and into the camp, followed by a rag-tag army of children pulling at the heavy parachutes.

As they passed the church, the Salvation Army band struck up a medley they had been secretly practising for such a day as this: national anthems which they had disguised with artful cunning in practice so that the guards could not guess their purpose. Now they were joyfully belted out for all to hear, and all to join in. In the midst of the pandemonium, the leader of the parachutists, Major Stanley Staiger, drew two pistols and pushed through the crowd to the guardhouse, where the Japanese commandant surrendered without resistance. He knew the war was over. Weihsien was liberated, and the only sadness that day was for those who had not lived to experience the taste of freedom. Among them, of course, Eric Liddell.

★ ★ ★

After Eric's death in February it took many weeks for the news to reach Scotland. It was received with shock and a widespread sense of loss, which was felt not just in the religious, rugby and university circles to which Eric had belonged, but on the football terraces, in the cinema queues and on the street corners, where once again his name was on the billboards.

'Scotland has lost a son who did her proud every hour of his life,' wrote the *Glasgow Evening News*.

The *Edinburgh Evening News* described him as 'one of the best known and most admired men who ever took part in sport, whose devotion to his principles won him the highest esteem.' In another article a leading sports writer summed him up as 'probably the most illustrious type of muscular Christianity ever known.' The newspapers were never short of a phrase, or a headline, where Liddell was concerned.

Memorial services were held in many parts of Scotland. In Glasgow, people packed into Dundas Street Congregational Church, where Eric's father had been ordained before leaving for China all those years before. All the leading churchmen were there, the heads of missionary societies, missionaries, students, sportsmen, D.P. Thomson, Eric's brother Rob (now home from China), his younger brother Ernest and his sister Jenny. There, too, was the manager of Rangers Football Club, the legendary Bill Struth, who could always count on an extra 10,000 at the gate at the annual Rangers Sports Meeting when Eric Liddell was running; Duncan (Dunky) Wright, the British marathon champion; John M. Bannerman, the Scottish rugby internationalist and champion of Gaeldom.

Alan Morton, one of Scotland's greatest footballers and darling of the terraces, read the lesson, and one by one the tributes were paid.

Bill Struth said:

> He deliberately sacrificed a fine chance of one Olympic title because of his religious convictions. He just as certainly put aside a career of brilliance and affluence to serve his master in the most practical of all forms of Christianity. In his work in China he created an opportunity for the

talents with which he was so richly endowed, courage, determination, skill, endurance and self-sacrifice, to be utilised to the full. Sport gave to Eric Liddell its highest honours; nevertheless, it is true to say that he honoured sport rather than sport honouring him.

The details of the last few years of his life are not yet known to us, but we can be certain that under the most severe of all trials, he exhibited just those qualities which he showed in his sporting life. His life was perhaps a short one; but his work, as he clearly saw it, and, as we believe, divinely inspired, carried out away from the applause of the crowd, will remain a source of inspiration to many.

Bill Struth concluded on a note which sounds uncannily modern:

> In these days of exaggerated hero-worship and publicity for sports champions, Eric Liddell's example reminds us to put things in their proper perspective. Sport to him was sport, not the be-all and end-all, and success in it did not prevent him from picking out the things spiritual from the things temporal. His was an example which must have helped others to make a similar choice.

Dunky Wright, Scotland's greatest long-distance runner, told the congregation:

> Eric was greater than an athlete; he was a crusader. He was without doubt the most glorious runner I have ever seen. Never has there been a greater need for a man with such a high moral and virile Christian character like Eric Liddell to be set as an example to our young people. I would suggest that a picture of Eric Liddell be hung in every youth club and sports pavilion in our country, with the title, 'Eric Liddell: a Christian sportsman.'

The Revd Robert Dobbie, who had been one of the founders of the Scottish Student Campaign Movement in 1922, described him as 'a very parfit gentil knight.'

In Edinburgh, the service was in Morningside Congregational Church, where Eric had been a member in his student days. There were nearly 1,000 people present, including Eric's sister and two brothers. Among the speakers was George Robertson, Eric's old headmaster at Eltham College who was now head of George Watson's College, Edinburgh. Dunky Wright spoke again, as did D.P. Thomson.

Across the world, in Toronto's Carlton Street United Church there were addresses by the Revd George King, who had been interned with Eric for six months, and the Revd T.T. Faichney, a Perthshire man who had been minister of the Union Church in Tientsin. Mr Faichney told the gathering, which included Florence and the girls:

> Everything that Eric did, he did well; he had a passion for perfection. For one who was among the world's fleetest of foot, I often marvelled that he was so slow in speech and in the things he did. But it was because nothing less than the best was good enough.

He held up a copy of *The Sermon on the Mount*, the collection of Sunday school lessons that Eric had published for the teachers of the Tientsin church when he was Sunday school superintendent: 'It is the best thing that I have on the Sermon on the Mount in my library. Going through it one marvels at his erudition, his wide reading and his spiritual perception.'

In Florence's letter to Thomas Cocker-Brown she wrote of feeling overwhelmed by the kindness of friends and strangers. Her heart ached for Jenny, Rob and Ernest, she said, and she wished they could have been at the Toronto memorial service the previous Saturday which had included such 'beautiful, sincere tributes' to Eric.

It was obvious to many that Eric's widow and children had been left in straitened circumstances. In Scotland a plan was quickly underway to help the family. A national committee was formed to launch the Eric Liddell Memorial Fund, with Sir Iain Colquhoun of Luss as chairman and all the great names in church and business, the universities and sport, on the committee. Fundraising functions were held up and down the country. Collections were taken at football matches, rugby grounds, sports meetings, fetes and charity balls. Business firms donated advertising space and money poured in from private contributions. Soon there was enough in the fund to educate Eric's three daughters and found the Eric Liddell Challenge Trophy for the best performance of the year in the Scottish Schools Athletic Association Championship meeting.

Dunky Wright used to coach boys for the championships, and he never failed to remind them of Eric's gold medal and how he came to win the 400 metres instead of the 100 metres. 'To win an Olympic event is a great honour,' he would tell them, 'perhaps the greatest athletic honour. But Eric Liddell is not remembered for this achievement, but the man who wouldn't run on a Sunday.'

An Eric Liddell Memorial Room was opened in the St Ninian's Conference and Training Centre in Edinburgh. Eltham College built a new boarding house and named it after him. The 3rd Hong Kong Sea Scout Group was just one of many scouting organisations to establish a Liddell Patrol. The Perthshire town of Crieff claimed to have the only Eric Liddell Boys' Club in the world, and eighteen months after his death there was a memorial service held by rugby enthusiasts in the Borders. There were thirteen Scottish Internationalists in St Paul's Parish Church, Galashiels, that day and D.P. Thomson told them:

> It's nearly twenty-one years since Liddell's athletic career in this country closed, and nearly a year and a half since he died. For what other athlete could such a gathering be assembled, in a town in which he has never lived, and a district to which he only paid one or two visits?

In *Rugger My Pleasure*, the sports writer A.A. Thomson summed up what the sporting world thought of Eric Liddell:

> During the worst period of his imprisonment he was, through his courage and cheerfulness, a tower of strength and sanity to his fellow prisoners. To many sufferers he brought the only comfort that captivity allowed. It is one of the deep sadnesses of life, that while so many survived the years of captivity, E.H. Liddell, who had helped so many, did not. He was one of the most chivalrous of Scots, as an athlete and as a man.

Since the Second World War, Eric Liddell has been the subject of magazine and newspaper articles, and radio and television programmes. Sunday school courses have been based on his life, church congregations have listened to sermons about him. An Eric Liddell strip cartoon even found its way into the pages of a boys' comic. In Edinburgh, the Eric Liddell Centre is a living memorial to the man, providing a range of community services for the most vulnerable in society, as well as carers and young people. Its credo, like that of the man it is named after, is acknowledging 'the infinite value and potential of each unique human being.'

The University of Edinburgh, the *alma mater* which celebrated Liddell's Olympic triumph so exuberantly in 1924, has continued to honour his memory. In 1991 the university paid for the erection of a handsome memorial stone near his grave in what is now the city of Weifang. A slab of warm pink granite quarried from the Isle of Mull was shipped out to

Cartoon from *The Victory*. (D.C. Thomson and Co. Ltd, Dundee)

China, where the authorities at Weifang had prepared a small Garden of Inspiration in his honour.

On the steaming hot Sunday of 9 June 1991, around forty people from half a dozen countries arrived in Weifang for a small ceremony to mark the unveiling of the stone on the site of the former internment camp.

Some, like David Michell and Norman Cliff, had known Eric Liddell as children in the camp; his brother Rob's daughter, Dr Peggy Judge from Edinburgh, represented his family; also from Edinburgh came Charles Walker, who had initiated the idea of this memorial stone through the Eric Liddell Foundation charity, formed to bring together young people from Hong Kong, China and the UK in educational endeavours. The Scotsmen's kilts swung briskly as the party walked through the dusty, cobbled streets of Weifang, following a similarly kilted piper who treated the bemused Chinese onlookers to an invigorating blast of Scotland the Brave along the way.

The foreign band wound its way past red flags and revolutionary slogans, mingling with a welcoming party of girls in red skirts and pristine white blouses and a group of young Chinese trumpeters. They entered the little garden which had been specially created near Eric's unmarked grave on the site of what is now Weifang's Second Middle School. There in the centre of the garden was the two-metre high stone, covered in crimson cloth. To the retort of Chinese firecrackers, Peggy Judge and the vice-mayor of Weifang city unveiled the stone.

At the top of the stone is etched a Celtic cross and at the foot the crest of the University of Edinburgh. Below the name ERIC H. LIDDELL stands a description of his life in English and then Chinese. It reads:

ERIC LIDDELL WAS BORN IN TIANJIN
OF SCOTTISH PARENTS IN 1902. HIS
CAREER REACHED ITS PEAK WITH HIS
GOLD MEDAL VICTORY IN THE 400
METRES EVENT AT THE 1924 OLYMPIC
GAMES. HE RETURNED TO CHINA TO WORK
IN TIANJIN AS A TEACHER. LIDDELL WAS
INTERNED IN A CAMP AT THE PRESENT SITE
OF THE WEIFANG SECOND MIDDLE SCHOOL AND
DIED IN THIS CAMP SHORTLY BEFORE THE
JAPANESE WERE DEFEATED IN 1945. HE
EMBODIED FRATERNAL VIRTUES, AND HIS
WHOLE LIFE WAS SPENT ENCOURAGING YOUNG
PEOPLE TO MAKE THEIR BEST CONTRIBUTIONS
TO THE BETTERMENT OF MANKIND.

Both the memorial stone and the dedication ceremony itself were delicate compromise between the communist scruples of the hosts a the Christian beliefs of the man they were there to honour. Only two years after the bloody suppression of a democratic uprising in Beijing's Tiananmen Square, the Chinese authorities were adamant that there should be no overt Christian expression in the honouring of Eric Liddell: no hymns, no mention of God. The speeches in the garden and the words on the stone were carefully phrased to emphasise the 'fraternal virtues' to which both hosts and guests could pay due honour; Liddell's commitment to young people was mutually celebrated.

But on the back of the stone are inscribed two further lines which would surely not have been there if the authorities had realised their provenance, two lines of poetry in which Eric's whole life is secretly distilled. They are the words from the Bible on which the fictional Eric Liddell preaches so eloquently in *Chariots of Fire*, the words of Isaiah the prophet which speak, to those who know the context, not about athletic endeavour or the betterment of mankind at all, but about those who wait upon the Lord:

> THEY SHALL MOUNT UP WITH WINGS AS EAGLES;
> THEY SHALL RUN AND NOT BE WEARY.

Epilogue

David Puttnam was lying ill in a rented house in Los Angeles. His last film *Midnight Express*, the story of a drug trafficker in a Turkish prison, had come out in 1978 and left him with a sour taste in his mouth. A shattering exposition of human nature at its most bestial, it was a film he knew to be cynical, and its instant triumph at the box-office and with the critics disillusioned him. The acclaim he now enjoyed as Britain's most successful film-maker had brought him little joy. He had a string of movies behind him already, including the award-winning *Bugsy Malone*, *The Duellists*, *That'll Be the Day* and *Brother, Can You Spare a Dime?* But the taste of success was not as sweet as he had imagined. He was ready now to make a film that was different.

In the library of his rented home, he casually picked up a book to while away the time; it was *The Official History of the Olympic Games* by Bill Henry. In it was something that seized his attention. In the chapter on the 1924 Olympics in Paris he read this:

Undoubtedly the dark-horse honours of the 1924 games went to E.H. Liddell, a bandy-legged little Scottish divinity student who, driven from his favourite event, the 100 metres, by his religious scruples, which prevented him from running on Sunday, surprised himself and everybody else by winning the 400 metres in record time.

Liddell, an awkward runner who obviously was unfamiliar with the distance, set out like a scared jackrabbit at the sound of the gun and fought off the challenge of H.M. Fitch of the United States down the stretch to cover the distance in 47⅗ seconds. Not satisfied with this performance, he was a good third in the 200 metres, which was won by Jackson Scholz of the United States.

As Puttnam was to discover from subsequent research, this account of Liddell's exploits at the Paris Olympics was not entirely accurate (Liddell was a science student at the time, for instance, and the 200 metres came before the 400 metres); but by now his imagination had been well and truly fired. His next movie was born, *Chariots of Fire*, which was to become one of Britain's most enduringly popular and successful films, winning four Oscars, including the coveted Best Picture.

Speaking just before *Chariots of Fire* went on general release in 1981, to an acclaim he could only dream of as he talked that day, Puttnam said: 'I am always reading that kind of book and I couldn't understand why I hadn't come across this tale before. It read for me like a wonderful *Boys' Own* story. I wanted to find out more.'

As he delved further into the history of the Paris Olympics, Puttnam also developed an interest in the figure of Harold Abrahams, the Jewish student who had won the 100 metres gold medal after Eric Liddell declined to take part. With that, the idea for a film began to take shape. The dramatic potential in the complementary lives of the two men began to excite him. Liddell and Abrahams were so different, in background, temperament, religion and motivation. And they were the fastest runners in the world.

'We live in such an expedient society,' Puttnam said. 'I have felt that for a long time. I became more and more interested in people who choose not to be expedient, and it seemed that sport could be a wonderful metaphor, a more accessible metaphor than religion in, for instance, Robert Bolt's *A Man for All Seasons*.'

He looked around for the kind of script-writer whose work would reflect the spirit of the idea he had in mind, and he hit at last upon Colin Welland, the actor, who had starred in *Z Cars* and *Kes* before becoming an author and playwright. Welland had written the original screenplay of the film *Yanks*, and a succession of award-winning television plays such as *Roll On Four O'Clock*, *Leeds United*, *Kisses at Fifty* and *Your Man from Six Counties*.

'There is something heroic about Colin Welland's writing,' said David Puttnam. 'It occasionally goes over the top, but it is marvellous, unembarrassed, heroic writing. And that is what we needed. I gave him the material.'

Colin Welland went wading into the research with enthusiasm, poring for months over diaries, books, newspaper cuttings and papers in order to get inside the skin of Eric Liddell.

'I got to know Eric Liddell essentially by reading about him a great deal and talking about him to people who had known him,' said Welland.

'But in particular I was hugely helped by a young man who had never actually met him – he's far too young – but has more or less modelled his life on him.'

The man who was so helpful to Colin Welland in his search for Eric Liddell was John Keddie, a thirty-four-year-old London Scot, born and brought up in Edinburgh. Keddie was an outstanding member of Edinburgh Southern Harriers in the 1960s; he won the Scottish Junior Triple Jump championship and was runner-up in the 400 metres. At the age of nineteen, when he was competing on the senior athletics circuit, his brother, who later became a minister in the USA, sent him a booklet about Liddell 'to encourage me to become more involved in spiritual things and get a better balance in my life'. John Keddie was so impressed by the Liddell story that he not only joined an evangelical Christian group but refused to take part in the Sunday meetings of the Scottish Amateur Athletics League.

Had that affected his athletics career?

No, I don't think I was ever going to be the greatest, but I was one of the key runners then, and when another chap and I refused to run I think our club persuaded the league to change to Saturday meetings. But it was Liddell's example that gave me the courage to stand my ground. Once I had done it I was able to take a much more balanced view of running. It ceased to be the be-all and end-all of my life. I became a really committed Christian and a keen supporter of Sunday observance. I even worked for the Lord's Day Observance Society for some years as an accountant. I made a complete survey of Liddell's life and published it in the Athletics Weekly. That's why I was able to help Colin Welland with details. I don't know that I would go as far as to say that I modelled my life on Eric Liddell's, but he certainly had a powerful influence in redirecting my life.

John Keddie was able to tell Welland a great deal about Liddell. He described how he preached, how he expressed himself and the things he wouldn't say as well as the things he did. Welland said:

For instance, John Keddie told me that Eric would never say 'Good luck!' He didn't believe in chance, but in Providence. Now, I would almost certainly have had Eric saying 'Good luck!' in the pre-race sequences, when he went around shaking hands with the other contestants and wishing them well. I can't remember what I have him saying – 'All the best!' or something like that – but certainly not 'Good luck!'

Welland found Liddell a very appealing character:

> All the more so when I went to meet his sister in Edinburgh, and people like the lady who had been his great schoolgirl fan, Mrs Elsa Watson. What came through was a picture of someone very cheery, full of fun and tricks, very chirpy, not at all sanctimonious. I never got the impression at any time of 'wetness'. Anyone who could stand up to the athletics establishment as he did isn't wet.
>
> I'm sure there are still men like Liddell around, but probably not in sport. Top sportsmen aren't usually like that. They have their principles up to a point, but there is also this compelling urgency to make their success before they pass their peak, and so they swallow their principles and go off to compete in South Africa, or in Moscow, or wherever. It's very rare to find anyone who would give up what Liddell did, just for the sake of a principle.

But Eric Liddell also provided problems for the script-writer. Drama thrives on inner conflict, family dissension, last-minute surprises: Liddell's decision not to run on a Sunday had none of these. So Welland wrote some disapproval into the part of Eric's sister, Jenny; he compressed the Olympic timetable and had Liddell discovering only on his way to Paris that the heats of the 100 metres were to be on a Sunday; he introduced Jenny and Eric's brother Rob as spectators in Paris, when they were both actually in China at the time; he invented a race between Liddell and Abrahams, the race which actually would have taken place if Abrahams had not developed a septic throat at the AAA Championships at Stamford Bridge in 1923. Another problem arose when Douglas Lowe, winner of the 800 metres for Great Britain in the 1924 Olympics, declined to cooperate with the film-makers: Welland had to invent a fictitious character instead, a dilettante aristocrat who emerged from his pen as a hurdler, not an 800 metres man. This was Lord Linsey in the film, fictitious winner of the silver medal in the 400 metres hurdles.

But it was only in the details of the story that the film-makers allowed themselves the luxury of improving on history. The personalities of the two men were sacrosanct; they were to be represented exactly as research showed them to have been. David Puttnam watched the research developing, with mounting fascination:

Liddell and Abrahams became more and more interesting because it became more and more clear that here was the chance to do a film about the two 'mes'. Abrahams is me as I am: rather driven. And Liddell is the man I would like to be and try to pretend that I am.

They represent two attitudes to victory. Abrahams gets little out of winning; he ends up feeling sick. The winning wasn't worth the effort. Liddell does it out of a sense of love: running for him is its own *raison d'être*.

But Puttnam's friends were sceptical of what he was trying to do. No contemporary audience would be able to understand anyone refusing to run for Liddell's reason, they said. Puttnam was rattled. He still believed it would work, but found it impossible to explain to anybody why he thought so. In the end, after the casting, he realised the missing factor was simply the performance of the actor in the part. He would either carry the conviction of the role, or he would not. When he saw Ian Charleson in the role he knew he had the man he needed.

Charleson was a young Scottish actor, born and brought up in Edinburgh, where he attended the Royal High School and, by happy coincidence, Edinburgh University. He studied architecture there to begin with, and then, when he found himself developing an interest in acting, switched to an MA degree. After graduating, he won a place at the London Academy of Music and Dramatic Arts. Thereafter, he joined the Young Vic, playing Guildenstern in Tom Stoppard's *Rosencrantz and Guildenstern are Dead*. He then played Hamlet with the Royal Cambridge Theatre's production, and followed this with a triumphant West End debut, playing a Glasgow lout in *Otherwise Engaged*.

Like David Puttnam and Colin Welland, Ian Charleson also spent long hours trying to understand Eric Liddell and come to grips with the mystery of his faith.

'It was an incredible faith,' Charleson said after the film was finished:

> I think it took precedence over everything – even over himself. In order to understand him, I read the Bible from beginning to end. I had to find something in the Christian faith that I could feel with him. And I found lots in it that is very true for anybody. There is some incredible wisdom in the Bible.
>
> When you are acting a part you have to take on as much of the character as you can. You have to find elements in yourself which you can use,

so that you can be real to yourself. I am a fairly easy-going person as a rule. I just used my nice side for the part and tried to suppress my baser instincts. I came across as just that: someone who is not a victim of his base instincts. Liddell was like that.

Charleson found his own personality changing for a time as he drew to the surface those elements that brought him close to Liddell: 'What I admired about him was his serenity. My whole personality changed during the time I was doing the part. I became very slow and laconic.'

The problem of making the simple goodness of Liddell's character interesting exercised him greatly:

> It was a great worry. What I was terrified of was playing a real goody-goody, the kind of person you want to punch because he is so bloody holy. But I discovered that he wasn't like that. He is interesting. It's this faith of his again. Anyone who can believe that strongly in something and not push it as a dogma, and not use it as a crutch for his life, has got to be interesting.
>
> The way I see it, he never pushed his faith down anyone's throat. When he spoke, he spoke rather quietly. He just talked about real things – about himself and his faith and what he did that morning.

Playing the part of Liddell gave Ian Charleson something important:

> I learned a lot from the man. That may sound corny, but it's true. You can't read the Bible with the kind of care I did without learning something yourself. I don't know if I believe in a supreme God the way Eric did, but it makes a lot of sense. For instance, there's a bit in the Bible that really impressed me – all about it not being that which goes into a man that defiles him, but that which comes out. That really made me think.

Ian Charleson died, tragically early himself, on 6 January 1990, of Aids. He was forty. Desperately ill and knowing he was dying, he had taken the demanding role of Hamlet at the National Theatre in London and given what was hailed as the finest performance of his life. Of his last night on stage, on 13 November 1989, his fellow actor Ian McKellen wrote:

> His voice was firm and sweet. The soliloquies are where Hamlets generally fail but Ian spoke them like conversations on life and death, and shrank the vast auditorium to the intimacy of a drawing-room. That would have

been remarkable under any circumstances but as his throat was physically distorted and his lungs impaired, we were witnessing a near miracle of will and energy.

'O that this too too sullied flesh would melt Thaw and resolve itself into a dew.'

He covered his face with his thin, white hands. Hamlet was effortlessly aware of his own mortality and, without sentimentality or self pity, [Charleson] made us all aware that young men, princes, actors – all of us – must die. Hamlet's journey to the fulfillment of the last scene, when he is ready to face his destiny, was clearly charted.

During the last weeks of his life, Ian Charleson often talked about Hamlet, but he also talked of Eric Liddell. Indeed David Puttnam believes that his experience in embodying Liddell as an actor became crucially important at the end. He told the BBC World Service *Omnibus* programme in 1991 that Ian had died with extraordinary grace:

> It was very, very remarkable to be around him. And it would be nice to think that during what must have been agonising months for him both physically and emotionally, in some way Eric, or having been Eric, or Lord knows what he did for Eric, was a significant help to him.

It seems that near the end Ian Charleson did indeed feel exceptionally close to Eric Liddell. His parents Jack and Jean Charleson, who lived in Edinburgh, told Eric's niece Peggy Judge that as he lay dying, their son was reaching out for the man whose mind and soul he had plumbed so avidly just a few years previously. Who can tell what he found in those last days and hours of life. Perhaps the man who so beautifully caught the essence of Eric Liddell on film also mounted up on eagle-wings in death.

And thus the fragrance of Eric Liddell's life has continued to spread down the years, affecting all sorts of unlikely people. At Weifang in China his influence is still reverberating sixty years after his death. During the ceremony to dedicate the memorial stone in 1991, there was a break in the overcast clouds and for a fleeting minute or two, a shaft of light played over the garden of remembrance. A Chinese official suddenly tugged at the sleeve of Charles Walker from Edinburgh with a shy comment which amazed him: 'See. God has put in an appearance for Mr Eric.' At the sixtieth anniversary celebrations on the same spot in 2005, it did not seem a ridiculous hope that the Liddell effect would be rippling as far as the Beijing Olympics in 2008.

In the Western world, to a society which worships both easy celebrity and anti-heroism, Eric Liddell is a puzzling anomaly. What are we to make of a life that comprehended both drive and serenity, will to achieve and the grace to give in, absolute principles and utter humanity, charisma and ordinariness? A society which thinks itself too clever for religion may struggle to understand Eric Liddell, but nobody has come into contact with that life, then or now, without realising that the secret lay in the resources he tapped when his head jerked back and he ran blind, and with the spiritual source to which he surrendered when the final race was over. In that sense, it is no secret at all.

If you are interested in purchasing other books published by Stadia, or in case you have difficulty finding any Stadia books in your local bookshop, you can also place orders directly through the Tempus Publishing website

www.tempus-publishing.com